The False Peace

Why The Abraham Accords Cannot Protect The Gulf From A Radicalised Israel

Miriam Goldstein

Global East-West (GEW) London

Copyright © 2025 by Miriam Goldstein

Collection: Geopolitics

Global East-West (GEW) London

All rights reserved.

No portion of this book may be reproduced in any form without written permission from the publisher or author, except as permitted by copyright law.

Contents

Introduction   1

1. The Doctrine of Reoccupation   19
2. The Crumbling Accords   37
3. Strategic Encirclement: Turkey and Iran   53
4. The Target is the Gulf   69
5. Geopolitics of the 'Greater Israel'   87
6. Normalisation as Subjugation   103
7. Surveillance and Sovereignty: The Israeli Nexus   119
8. The Diplomatic Facade: A Look Behind Closed Doors   137
9. The Role of the International Community   157
10. Building a Cohesive Arab Strategy   175

Introduction
The Illusion of Containment

Historical Background and Development of the Doctrine of Containment

The evolution of containment strategies has historical antecedents in the divided geopolitics of the post-war era and represents a persistent legacy for contemporary territorial disputes. After World War II, there was a fundamental shift in global power that necessitated the requirement of new security doctrines. The wider dissemination of communist beliefs and the growing influence of the Soviet Union saw Western powers, led by the United States, enact what would later be referred to as the containment policy. The goal of this policy was to stop the spread of communism, especially in Europe and East Asia, and prevent it from infiltrating more states. One such element of containment was the Marshall Plan, which sought to provide financial assistance to war-damaged countries, stopping them from turning communist or otherwise forming dissenting allegiances. With time, the idea of containment expanded beyond military and diplomatic aspects to include economic, cultural, and social ones. It turned into a model for international relations, defining alliances and divisions and determining how to resolve conflicts. The logic of containment also encourages states to work together in forming alliances such as NATO and SEATO, and it remains a persistent factor that shapes global governance arrangements through cooperative security mechanisms. Containment has also been directly linked to various local conflicts, as superpowers applied it to anticipate and manage the powers of other nations, while entropy refers to the change and competition between different political ideologies. The Cuban Missile Crisis is a classic case/instance, emphasising the proximity of containment and Soviet infiltration of military power on this side of the United States. Moreover, the tradition of containment is echoed today in current debates about interventionism, deterrence, and multilateral agreements. Current discussions about the prevention of nuclear proliferation, cyber warfare, and asymmetrical threats illustrate its continuing relevance. Through exploring the historical origins and early deployment of containment, we can develop a far richer understanding of its complexities, contradictions, and long-lasting implications for world politics.

The Illusion Defined: False Sense of Security

The idea of containment, which primarily aims to confront and manage geopolitical threats based on the principle that isolation can sufficiently limit an enemy's ability to cause serious harm, has actually informed the 89-6 rule. But this myth, however influential it was in the past, has proved to be a mirage all too often recently and has lulled key players on the international scene into a false sense of security. The idea that containment could sequester potential enemies behind a metaphorical iron curtain and the world would be safe from their influence has been tripping up policy planners for decades. We must break apart this false impression and accept the weakness of such a course.

Essentially, the illusion of containment is nothing more than a fallacy that control over paper lines on a map or military encirclement can overcome an opposing party with unwavering resolve. This reductive approach, however, fails to account for the fluid nature of contemporary war and the myriad ways in which adversaries might leverage weakness. The modernisation of technology, the globalisation of the economy, and asymmetric tactics have reduced the effectiveness of conventional containment methods.

Additionally, the erosion of traditional battlefields and the increase of cyber and information warfare have made physical barriers less clear in stopping threats. <Nations pursuing containment without recognising the reality of these changes can never escape perpetuating reactionarily driven defences that fail to address the root sources and causes of war.</Nations>

The misconception that isolation alone can lessen regional consequences and vulnerabilities adds to the illusion of containment. In actuality, the effects of containment are not limited to a particular state or entity; it affects entire regions and global stability. The growing interdependence of the international system means that efforts to control a specific actor can reverberate across territorial boundaries.

Economic disturbances, rising tensions, and misguided strategic partnerships are just a few examples of the complex web of side effects resulting from what are perceived as containment efforts.

And, accordingly, it must be understood that containment as insulating a state or region from external threats could counterintuitively lead to more uncontrollable instability and consequent adversarial behaviour. In dismantling the illusion of containment, it is urgent to move toward comprehensive and complex approaches to global problem sets. This project aims to challenge and dismantle the myth of containment to re-examine phase-locked assumptions about US foreign policy as it moves toward a much fuller paradigm suited to the realities of modern-day geopolitics.

Global Actors and Regional Consequences

The structure of the current system is determined by a number of actors as well as their numbers and interactions, each with its own political, economic and military power. At the centre of this intricate web of impact are the regional implications following the moves and ploys made by these players. The effects of their engagements ripple across borders, affecting power relations, security, and stability in the regions that are put under close examination and far beyond them as well. In the Middle East, global powers (the US, Russia, China, and the EU) have resulted in a power binary. Their diplomatic efforts, military incursions and economic forays reverberate across the region, too often alienating allies or forging unexpected alliances. The interests pursued by these actors generate opportunities and challenges for the states and non-state actors in the field. Moreover, the diffusion of transnational players and regional actors calls for a more complex understanding of the degree to which contemporary conflicts are interconnected. The geopolitical implications of energy policies, the complexities around international arms sales, and the stakes of world powers will be much more important for peace and stability in the region. In order to achieve this, it is crucial to examine the motivations and strategies of these players, who frequently play a dual role in shaping the fates of nations and peoples caught in today's complex interactions between empires. Furthermore, the increasing number of non-state actors such as transnational terrorist groups and insurgencies further complicates the already complex web of global and regional interactions. Much of the power and influence posed by these non-state actors (which often have external sponsorship, including transnational ideologies) are undermining traditional paradigms focused on the state. Therefore, the collision between international and domestic interests determines the rising of new power relationships, challenging sovereignty and territorial integrity norms. The interactions and overlaps between global and regional players are crucial for fully understanding the complexities of current conflicts, which transcend traditional boundaries and challenge the concept of a classical sphere of influence.

The Unravelling of Strategic Alliances

Alliance formation has always been a key feature of global diplomacy and the balance of power. But these alliances have unraveled at breakneck speed in recent years, including within our particular geographical area of interest. A complex lattice of partnerships and accords that had underwritten the region's security and cooperation has fallen apart in the face of growing pressures at one end and competing priorities at the other. Strategic alliances were born in response to mutual threats or goals. Whether based on formal treaties or loose understandings, these partnerships were characterised by shared commitment and mutual reliance. However, we are witnessing a new phase where former friends rethink their loyalties and the strategic calculus of all parties is changing. Multi-hinges are the catalysts for this unravelling. One established alliance after another is disintegrating due to realigned power structures, shifting threat perceptions and new leaders. In addition, the rise of non-traditional security threats and the militarisation of economic interdependence have placed new pressure on these seemingly strong ties. Nor can one ignore the competition between rival ideologies and competing geopolitical agendas, which undermines strategic cooperation. The conflicting interests of traditional and rising powers have exacerbated fault lines within these alliances, leading to divergences that could weaken regional stability. In addition, trust and confidence between the former friends have deteriorated, making the disintegration of these strategic alliances even worse. Cases of alleged betrayal, unilateral decision-making, and behind-the-scenes deals have created paranoia and mistrust, undermining partnerships' protocols. As we make our way through this shifting alliance maze, it is quite necessary that we come to understand the impact of this unravelling on regional security, economic well-being and geopolitical factors. The collapse of long-standing strategic partnerships has led to a period of growing uncertainty, requiring a fresh account and new tasks for managing risks. This is a chapter I hope to unpack in some of its complexity, going through the genealogy as well as moments that unfold for us now. By dissecting the phenomenon through a collection of works, we provide an explanation to determine its intricate nature and implications, insights crucial for understanding the changing world in global politics.

Economic Dimensions of Regional Tensions

The economic aspects of the regional confrontations are intricate and multi-dimensional, reshaping the frames of geopolitical rivals in the involved countries. Resource distribution imbalances, trade deficits and financial interdependencies are all issues that could escalate existing disputes to the detriment of international diplomacy. Structural factors like power games over oil, gas, and water can reignite old rivalries and reshape the power map. The competition for vital resources has the potential to intensify regional tensions, which are already on the verge of economic conflict, and cause significant damage to the global economy. In addition, trade deficits and economic inequality between countries can lead to skewed power relations and the possibility for exploitation from dominant economic players. Such inequalities can create mutual suspicion and enmity, increasing the potential for conflict and undermining attempts to resolve these matters diplomatically. Financial interdependence in the region intensifies tensions by subjecting countries to external economic power and sanctions. Economic isolation or collapse can exert a coercive influence on decision-making, accelerate hostilities, and perpetuate regional disunity. In addition, economic interests fanned through strategic alliances and international relations introduce an added dimension of intrigue in regional dynamics when states are caught between competing economic affiliations and seek to steer clear of political dependence. The fallout on regional economies, employment, and lifestyles also shows the strong implications of economic aspects in inter-regional strife. Perhaps most importantly, recognising the economic drivers of regional strife is critical when crafting holistic policies that confront their sources and work toward lasting peace and growth.

Technological Warfare and Information Control

In this age of constantly shifting geopolitical influence, technological warfare and information manipulation have taken centre stage as vital elements of global power play. The military's strategic application of superior technologies has subverted old ideas about warfare and given birth to a new period in which cyber capabilities, unmanned systems, and space assets would considerably affect the world power order. As they strive for advantages in this digital battlefield, they have seamlessly integrated "information control" with tactical objectives. The military can shape perceptions, guide perspectives, and conduct covert operations in the cyber domain, creating a new form of war that has no physical limits. At the core of this technological warfare, dominance has no bounds in cyberspace. In response, governments engage in a constant battle to safeguard their vital systems and communications, all the while infiltrating enemy networks to spy on them. But this hidden realm of competition has enhanced the role that cybersecurity plays as an element of national security, leading to significant investments in defensive capabilities and offensive cyber-based operations. Additionally, the convergence of AI, machine learning, and quantum computing has precipitated a change in how wars are fought, allowing algorithmic warfare and autonomy to define the future battlefield. At the same time, information warfare has become a powerful tool to shape perceptions and decision-making at global levels. The widespread adoption of social media and communications technology has given our adversaries new avenues to spread disinformation, engage in influence operations, and foment conflict among target populations. The use of information as a weapon, including covert propaganda and deepfake technology and the practice of psychological operations, confronts democratic societies with serious challenges, adding new complexities to modern conflicts. The war for information dominance has expanded beyond traditional diplomacy, affecting all aspects of our lives. This enormous danger of technology, warfare, and control is really a problem not only for the military but also spills over into all aspects of modern-day life. In this confusing landscape, understanding the interdependence between technology, information and strategic interests is key to making sense of the complexities of tech-age geopolitics.

Societal Impacts: Public Perception and Reality

When examining the complex dynamics of societal impacts within the context of regional tensions, it becomes imperative to scrutinise the intricate interplay between public perception and ground realities. The way in which the populace perceives and processes unfolding events is a critical facet that influences the socio-political landscape. At times, public sentiment can serve as a barometer for gauging the effectiveness of diplomatic measures and governmental actions. Furthermore, the role of media amplifies this influence, shaping public opinion through selective presentation of information and narrative framing. Hence, it is essential to delve into how these factors intersect with the broader conflict dynamics. Ground realities often diverge from public perception, illustrating the nuances embedded within complex geopolitical scenarios. As such, insular societal narratives and politicised rhetoric may distort the actual ramifications of policies and geopolitical manoeuvrings. These distortions can have tangible repercussions, both domestically and internationally, perpetuating misconceptions and hindering informed decision-making processes. Unravelling the layers of misperceptions and delving into the core realities is crucial for a comprehensive understanding of the societal impact. Moreover, societal impacts encompass not only the immediate region but extend to global perceptions of stability, security, and trust. A misalignment between public perception and ground realities can engender scepticism and erode confidence in international actors and institutions, thereby impeding collaborative conflict resolution efforts. The reverberations of such discordance resonate far beyond regional borders, influencing broader international relationships and alliances. Therefore, it is imperative to discern the prevailing societal impressions and address the disparities with adroit diplomacy and transparent communication. Equally significant is the examination of societal resilience in the face of adversities arising from regional tensions. In times of heightened geopolitical volatility, societies are subject to various stressors – economic, psychological, and emotional. Understanding the coping mechanisms and adaptive strategies employed by populations can shed light on the enduring impacts of prolonged conflicts. Additionally, exploring the role of societal pillars such as education, media, and civil society enhances comprehension of their resilience and capacity for positive change amidst adversity. Furthermore, socio-cultural shifts and identity dynamics are profoundly influenced by regional tensions and conflict narratives. These tumultuous undercurrents affect individual and collective narratives, shaping national identity and community cohesion. Studying the societal fabric within the purview of these shifts becomes pivotal for recognising and addressing emerging challenges and opportunities. By understanding how regional tensions affect social structures, policymakers and other interested parties can come up with smart solutions that meet the needs and wants of society.

Analysing Policy Failures and Miscalculations

Policy failures and miscalculations in the realm of geopolitics have the potential to reverberate across societies, economies, and global relations with profound consequences. In the context of containment strategies, it becomes imperative to scrutinise and dissect the specific instances where policies have faltered or been based on flawed assessments. One such critical examination involves evaluating the impact of interventionist approaches that often result in unforeseen geopolitical entanglements. Furthermore, the failure to anticipate the organic evolution of regional dynamics, coupled with a myopic focus on immediate objectives, has often led to strategic missteps and unintended repercussions. At the heart of many policy failures lies an overreliance on static assessments and an underestimation of the adaptive capabilities of regional actors. History is replete with examples of foreign interventions predicated on a misplaced optimism about the manageability of complex geopolitical scenarios. These ventures, far from achieving their intended goals, have frequently exacerbated existing tensions and volatility. It is essential to delve into the root causes of such misjudgments, which often stem from a combination of inadequate intelligence, ideological biases, and a lack of comprehensive understanding of historical grievances and sociocultural complexities. Moreover, the pursuit of unilateral policies without due consideration for multilateral engagement has often resulted in diplomatic isolation and alienation from potential allies. The disconnect between espoused values and realpolitik considerations has further undermined the credibility and efficacy of containment strategies. A retrospective analysis of such policy failures reveals poignant lessons about the dangers of hubris and the perils of disregarding the agency of local populations and non-state actors in shaping the course of events. Additionally, miscalculations stemming from an insistence on viewing the regional landscape through narrow ideological prisms rather than through pragmatic, nuanced lenses have significantly constrained the effectiveness of containment efforts. This dogmatic approach has inhibited the cultivation of meaningful dialogue and cooperation with divergent stakeholders, perpetuating cycles of animosity and obstructing constructive conflict resolution. Ultimately, an in-depth scrutiny of policy failures and miscalculations is indispensable for refining and reformulating future containment strategies. It is imperative to heed these cautionary tales as we navigate the intricate currents of global affairs, recognising that the pursuit of lasting stability demands a holistic, context-sensitive approach that transcends short-term expediency.

A Retrospective on Past Strategies

The tactics used by global and regional powers have always been a major factor in world affairs, often with grave consequences for nation states. A look back on the historical strategy offers us precious insights into this complex chain of decisions, actions and impacts. Points of control have been continuously established in global territories since the decline of colonial empires, creating highly calculated vampire economies where individual deaths serve as payment for backroom currency slights. Looking back at those strategies provides interesting insights into how historical events have shaped the region as it is today. Examining the past enables us to fully evaluate the achievements, inadequacies, and unexpected outcomes of various actors' actions. It reveals patterns of behaviour, themes, and problems that persistently shape current events. And it reveals how the central dynamics of power, allegiances and conflict in the region have developed. A thorough examination of previous strategies is necessary to develop knowledge- and future-based policy that considers the challenge of the depths in a politically nuanced and complex world. An examination of these motivations, rationales, and assumptions associated with past strategies provides a useful set of lessons for policymakers, analysts, and strategists. An astute retrospective can serve as a compass to navigate the complexities of current challenges by unveiling historical context, decision-making processes, and geopolitical calculations. In addition, it promotes a deeper understanding of the long-lasting legacies, unresolved tensions, and enduring aspirations that still shape the strategic calculus of the region. Dissecting the layers of past policies reveals a competition between different interests, security needs, and ideological anchorages as constitutive factors of regional behaviour. This rearview mirror exercise forces the reader to think about "what might have been" and at what point world events took a different turn in shaping global affairs. As such, it sets out an approach to comprehending the ongoing challenges, developing trends, and future possibilities of recasting regional dynamics. We need to bring back the wisdom gathered from a review of past strategies so that we can have subtlety, adaptability, and recognition of multi-dimensionality in today's geopolitics. It sets the stage for a rigorous exploration of historical antecedents, policy residues, and strategic dislocations that still echo through the region.

Preparing for Further Analysis

Setting the stage for subsequent analysis requires us to start by unravelling the intricate web of complexities that have shaped and built previous strategies. A historical overview of the regional dynamics, from diplomatic exchanges to military build-up, offers a panoramic view of this complex geopolitical terrain. Deciphering how former alliances, hostilities and power plays intertwine is key to making sense of where we are today and what's to come next.

Let's take a look at critical policy decisions that had much more profound implications than originally intended. Hindsight allows us to see the subterranean impulses and mistakes hidden beneath those earlier decisions, lessons essential to shaping today's plans and tomorrow's policies. What's more, through an analysis of past interventions, successful and otherwise – and the actors who made them so – we can also learn important lessons about how global and regional forces interact to produce outcomes on the ground, where they might be weakest in a system or fissuring.

In addition, understanding the economic aspect of regional animosities is critical in order to draw the complex web of interests and interplay that make up the game board so symbolic of geopolitics. Resource rivalries, economic codependence, detours or blockades on the money trail—we know that such factors commonly play a spurring role in influencing nations to confront one another (or coproduce with one another). It is important to comprehend these economic eddies when forecasting possible future interactions and in finding paths toward reducing friction and facilitating mutually beneficial relationships.

A second important angle to pay attention to is the junction of techno-warfare and information suppression. The asymmetrical nature of warfare is being amplified by developments in cyber capabilities and artificial intelligence, which are changing the very shape of conflict through what Vish Abuwala calls an age in which non-traditional challenges present existential threats. Contending with these emergent paradigms requires a surgical deconstruction of how technology influences the dynamics of power projection and national security at large, compelling policymakers and analysts alike to reorient their conventional axioms around these new realities for accurate recourse.

This is no time to ignore the socio-political consequences

of regional politics, as it is usually publics and societies whose perceptions and resilience help decide how long individual nations pass safely through turbulent times. Examining the delicate and potent influence of popular attitudes on foreign policy and domestic policies, we begin to understand the role of knowledge in energising or calming peoples. Sensitive to this importance, the evaluation of social responses to geopolitical trends becomes crucial from the viewpoint of prognosticating the durable constructiveness and effectiveness of strategic endeavours.

In conclusion, this initial review paves the way for future, in-depth studies to unravel the threads of historical, economic, technological, and societal factors that are woven into a complex tapestry of regional geopolitics. With this objective analysis we are making the stage ready to dissect carefully the policies of today and tomorrow in a manner that will enable you, dear readers, to understand these tangled threads and dynamic relations of integrated international politics.

1
The Doctrine of Reoccupation

Historical Overview of Reoccupation

The idea of reoccupation has a long history, which is partly responsible for contemporary thinking on how to reoccupy. Reoccupations have taken place throughout human history, usually with the intent of establishing a military presence on land that has previously been occupied or even strengthening control of regions that are considered strategically valuable.

One of the first mutations of reoccupation, which originated in Mesopotamia before the 4th century b.c., significantly predates the Allied Forces policy. Subsequent occupiers have wished to recover and expand their territorial area. The empires of the Assyrians, Babylonians and Persians, for example, all made use of the technique to assert their authority and prevent rebellion.

Likewise in the Mediterranean world, the activities of ancient Greece and Rome had, as their corollary, the reacquisition or reoccupation of lost or disputed territory. The Roman Empire's attempts to reoccupy territories such as Gaul and Britain demonstrate the critical importance of reoccupation as a political strategy.

With the progress of global discovery and conquest, reoccupation would also be characteristic of European imperial aspirations. During the Age of Discovery, European military dominance in warfare often enabled them to dominate indigenous people through disease, technology and warfare itself.

This context of history set the stage for the reoccupancy

practices inherited by modern states. In recent centuries, the reoccupation trend has taken on new aspects, notably as regards post-colonial designs and geopolitical competition. The established world infrastructure of reoccupation was shaped by both the consequences of World War II and the draw-line border politics in the Middle East that motivated nations to assert control over strategic resources and territories. What is more, the outbreak of the Cold War induced several reoccupations in which rival blocs competed to assert control over areas they regarded as vital spheres of interest. By mapping the evolution of reoccupation in historical perspective, this revelation highlights the way that territorial, political and economic imperatives have continued to inform strategies and motivations for attempts at reoccupation.

Legal and Political Justifications

There is a complex range of arguments about the legal and political justifications for reoccupation, and they fundamentally derive from historical issues, geopolitical factors, or diplomatic considerations. Legally speaking, those who support reoccupation often reference interpretations of international law that allow for the taking back of territory on the basis of history or for reasons of national security. Internationally educated lawyers and human rights advocates are always on hand to critique these assertions that breach established conventions or protocols. Proponents argue that reoccupation advances national interests and safeguards the people, even bringing some stability out of anticipated moments of fear. Such reasoning finds support from the diplomatic activities of tapping allies and partisans while hiding in the mesh of international relations and alliances.

Politically, justifications for reoccupation are extremely intermeshed with the broader picture of regional and global power. That's the reason why there is sharp contention over them. Advocates argue that reoccupation is a strategic move necessary to safeguard national interests, protect the citizens, and keep order against perceived threats.

Diplomatically, This logic is further supported by efforts to secure backing from allies and sympathisers, as well as by a complex network of international relations and rules. The political justifications for reoccupation often rest in the portrayal of it as a proactive measure either to fend off potential aggression or to reduce dangers coming from neighbouring entities. Drawing such a picture is certainly consistent with swelling public support at home and abroad for both military and diplomatic strategies to assert control over disputed or occupied territories. In addition to legal and political dimensions, economic slopes play a decisive role in the justifications for reoccupation.

Proponents argue that retaking territories opens up access to valuable resources, routes of trade, and economic opportunities vital for sustained national growth and weight. This kind of account is reinforced by appraisals of the economic dividends derived from territorial control and exploitation, which are treated as a key part of safeguarding the country's well-being and boosting its position in regional or international spheres. Thus, the legal and political justifications for reoccupation hold an overlapping network of conversations with myriad stakeholders. David understanding these aspects is crucial to apprehending the complexities and implications surrounding reoccupation as it engages across a broad spectrum of topics, such as those related to conflict resolution, diplomacy, international law/community standards.

Strategic Military Imperatives

The reoccupation framework is geographically incorporated into strategic military considerations. Despite any justifications for these assertions of legality and political claims, the doctrine undeniably retains the right to maintain and exercise military superiority over occupied lands. This chapter opens the complex strategic military imperatives on which reoccupation is based. First, we must establish the militarily important geographic location of the reoccupied territories. They commonly serve as important buffer zones or military positions, the most useful assets to control in terms of surveillance, defence and regional power. They are also taking into account historical precedents and lessons from previous occupations to determine their position within the invading hierarchy. They are confident that securing key military targets and strengthening defensive lines should be their primary priorities. Given the inter-relatedness of these imperatives with wider security policies, it would be prudent to conduct a full analysis of the military aspects of reoccupation.

More importantly, the ongoing drive for reoccupation provides a chance to recalibrate the regional balance of power and concentrate military power – missions that perfectly complement the long-term strategic objectives pursued by the concerned parties. Additionally, there is an issue regarding logistical infrastructure, supply lines, and the tactical positioning of forces that directly influence the sustainability and success of reoccupation prospects. Military exegesis and diplomatic manoeuvres.

The intertwinement of military imperatives with diplomacy highlights the complex relationship between coercive power and political ambition, where reoccupation embodies specific forms of strategic military imperatives. As a result, the high-stakes interplay between military imperatives and geopolitical ambitions creates a multi-layered fabric of challenges and prospects that demand a sophisticated appreciation of the game being played. As we probe the subtleties and nuances of strategic military requirements, it becomes apparent that a comprehensive understanding of these subtleties is critical in appreciating the complexities of reoccupation as a strategic goal.

Economic Motivations Behind Reoccupation

The wider political security calculations that drive state behaviour in conflict zones heavily influence reoccupation as an economic endeavour. Economic considerations are a critical factor that drive and sustain strategic objectives of the occupying power within the paradigm of domination. Whether it's dominance of oil and gas resources, dominance over trade routes, or creating economic dependencies—these agendas can offer important indications of the logic behind reoccupation.

The key to understanding the economic motivation for

reoccupation is the pursuit of resource control. The zones under occupation frequently contain large reservoirs of natural resources—such as oil, gas or raw materials—that can be very beneficial to the occupant's economy. By managing these resources, the occupying power can minimise dependency on external suppliers, protect its energy security, and increase its competitive position in surrounding markets. In addition to the straightforward material benefits of resource extraction, draining natural resources from an affected area seeks to undermine local economic stability and ability to support sustained resistance. Secondly, the establishment or reinforcement of economic dependencies may serve as motivation.

By incorporating the occupied territories in his economic sphere, he can take advantage of a captive market, profit from cheap labour and resources, and open channels for investment and trade that will serve his own economy to a greater degree than it would otherwise. This method not only uplifts the occupier economically but also amplifies its political power—as, based on economic interdependencies, it can use control and command cooperation with both local (domestic) constituencies and external agents.

Another significant economic factor is the strategy of trade routes that pass through these territories. Dominion over important trade routes, such as sea lanes, highways, or border crossings, may additionally provide leverage to help support and manage regional commerce. By controlling these arteries of trade, the occupier can govern the flow of goods and use influence to extend over wider economic fields, determine the economic fortunes of adjacent states by dint of its power, and rise to become a central player in the regional economy. Economic reasons for reoccupation are diverse and significant, ranging from resource management to economic dependency and control over trade routes. Understanding these reasons is vital for demystifying the complex array of interests on which reoccupation is based and exposing the delicate network that links economy, politics, and power relations in conflict areas.

Cultural and Ideological Factors

The cultural and ideological aspects contribute significantly to the phenomenon of reoccupation in this region. The Middle East has been shaped by centuries of ingrained cultural and religious stories, many of which have fuelled, rather than mitigated, territorial disputes or open conflict. The intricate network of multiple cultural and ideological factors significantly contributes to the endurance of tensions and the longevity of reoccupation policies. For one, historical entitlement is an important feature of cultural and ideological rationales for reoccupation. Many of the parties involved in these disputes have strong beliefs that this land is theirs, and they have texts, traditions, and narratives that are deeply rooted in its significance. Not only do these stories serve as touchstones to cultivate popular sympathy, but they also contribute to the development of a shared culture that heightens the significance of being an occupier.

Territorial claims further blur religious ideology along cultural lines. Certain sites and regions' religious mystique stirs emotions and reinforces the belief that defending the land is a sacred obligation. This merger has intertwined political goals with religious dictates, which has complicated the conflict. Cultural and ideological influences trickle down through society, affecting people's perceptions, attitudes and actions at the public level.

Cultural stories and school lessons perpetuate one historical and ideological interpretation, reinforcing the same divisions and nurturing resentment, suspicion and victimisation. This simply creates a vicious circle of hostility, from which it is difficult to develop reconciliation and durable peace between the two sides in the region. Adding to this entrenchment of reoccupation policies are, additionally, the use of cultural symbols, language and rituals as resistance or identity expression. The images and descriptions, the martyrological accounts—all of those play to the notion of occupation and resistance, strengthen it over time, harden us against them, and inhibit any possibility of cooperation and coexistence.

Finally, the weight of a vast and complex set of cultural and ideological influences should not be underestimated, which coalesce into a dense weave that supports, sustains and reproduces the cycle of reoccupation. It is essential to comprehend and address these complex dynamics in order to steer towards a sustainable solution that recognises and reconciles deeply entrenched cultural and ideological traits in the region.

Impact on Regional Power Dynamics

The competition for control and influence in the Middle East has always involved geopolitical, military, and ideological aspects. Reoccupation as a policy Indeed, the claim of reoccupation has implications for the current power balance and introduces new factors into an already complicated web of relations among competing regional actors. First, reoccupation changes the balance of power by strengthening the sense of legitimacy and audacity of the dispatching party. Such changes may, in turn, generate a shift in alliance and dependency patterns between states confronting the perceived threat or opportunity of the reoccupation.

The dominant strategy of the occupying power may, in addition, generate countervailing behaviour of other regional powers existing beforehand and then bring it into sharper relief. Moreover, regional power dynamics' implications reach beyond neighbours as distant players recalculate their policies and engagement in light of reoccupation. Key world players – and notably powers like the US, Russia, and China – could scale up or down their involvement in the region as a function of the changing balance of power and associated political-military risk-reward ratios. This realignment of external engagement can also serendipitously add complexity and texture to the regional power politics. Also, reoccupation brings the situation to a certain level of uncertainty and instability for power centres that are already present.

The looming threat of reoccupation, with its attendant military, political, and economic consequences, can condition the choices and actions of regional players, resulting in potential shifts in alliances, alignments, and projections of power. Such an environment can stoke or magnify historical resentments, territorial disputes, and old scores, causing a cascading effect throughout the region. The interrelationships of regional power dynamics also ensure that the impact of reoccupation extends beyond individual states or specific conflicts. Instead, it suffuses the Middle East region more generally and informs the strategic calculus, resource allocation, and security responses of all regional actors. Thus, understanding this metamorphosis is vital to grasping how the reoccupation doctrine will affect Middle Eastern power and what changes to expect.

International Response and Reactions

The world's response to the reoccupation doctrine has not been uniform, as so many interests and views are at stake. This response primarily involves striking a balance between diplomatic politics, geopolitical calculations, and values issues. One of the immediate international reactions was a quick denunciation of the reoccupation doctrine as yet another element that will cause instability in the region and possibly around the world. Powerful countries and international organisations have universally condemned aggressive reoccupation plans due to fears of violations of human rights, national sovereignty, and the subversion of established peace arrangements.

The United Nations has repeatedly expressed opposition to reoccupation practices, including through its organs and Security Council resolutions, and stressed that international law (and the rights of marginalised peoples) must be upheld. In addition to the diplomatic and political condemnations of reoccupation, global NGOs, human rights organisations, and movements have sprung into action to advocate against Israel's relentless colonisation project— based on its clear moral bankruptcy and humanitarian cost. Simultaneously, the response of major regional stakeholders has been a mixture of expressions of solidarity with affected populations, the pragmatic use of diplomatic opportunities, and, in some cases, hesitant support for proponents of reoccupation. The reactions of the neighbouring states have been coloured by their own complicated interests and histories with regard to the contested lands, resulting in a variety of positions between outright opposition and mute neutrality.

Secondly, different sectors, including energy markets, trade partners, and military allies, have reacted differently as the economic and security implications of reoccupation have begun to unfold. As Member States around the world wrestle with the complex array of challenges created by the doctrine of reoccupation, any use to promote constructive discussion, support conflict-resolution tools and uphold international norms is key in positioning themselves in reference to the ambiguous legal category. Ultimately, the developing global reaction and responses to the reoccupation doctrine highlight the complex interrelationship of geopolitics, morality, and collective security initiatives.

Comparative Analysis with Previous Occupations

Reoccupation has been a historical strategy in geopolitical conflicts. When we consider the details of earlier occupations, we may learn valuable lessons about the likely outcomes of current reoccupation doctrines. There are several important historical comparisons to consider. The repossessions of Alsace-Lorraine, East Prussia, and Sudetenland serve to illustrate how problems occur when trying to control lands once disputed. These experiences provide important testimony about the social, political, economic, and humanitarian effects of reoccupation.

Furthermore, the study of occupation within such decolonisation processes as those experienced with British rule in India or French rule over Algeria helps expose how lasting are the legacies and testimony for "lingering effects". Such testifying to "the continuing presence of a violence" is yet another way that prolonged territorialisation continues to speak out. Because these historical trajectories are key to policymakers and analysts trying to understand the possible implications for current reoccupation strategies.

Comparative study can provide a useful framework to evaluate the amount of international interventionism and complex power relationships developing within occupied territories. Additionally, it provides the reader with a significant shift in perspective regarding the persistent challenges of post-occupation transition and conflict resolution. It is of great value to analyse some aspects of reoccupation situations in order to elaborate the patterns and paradigms that might be useful for the understanding or intervention in present-day situations. This comparative perspective is equally key to assessing the implications and challenges of reoccupation in today's conflicts, shedding light on the multi-dimensional nature of these dynamics and leading to more nuanced policy and diplomatic responses.

Anticipated Consequences for Conflict Resolution

Prospective implications for conflict resolution in the realm of reoccupation are numerous and intricate. The reoccupation doctrine, although seemingly serving a particular interest at first glance, has an unparalleled impact on the resolution of the conflict in the region. The continued reoccupation ipso facto impugns the legitimacy of international efforts to work towards a fair and lasting settlement. It becomes a never-ending cycle of mistrust and hatred, making hopes for negotiations to work towards peace in the future ever more distant. In addition, the continued reoccupation of territory increases human suffering, worsens humanitarian crises, and increases human displacement and weakens social cohesion. The result has been a loss of trust and empathy between the combatants, increasing division as their attempts to resolve conflict grow more complex. The doctrine of reoccupation also creates an atmosphere where occupying forces commit human rights abuses and violate international law with apparent impunity. Such behaviour obstructs the creation of an atmosphere conducive to positive dialogue and detracts from the legitimacy of any future peace treaties.

Moreover, regardless of whether the economic wealth accrued in the occupied land is appropriated and controlled there, it risks perpetuating discrepancies between economies, which can lead to structural inequalities that are not conducive to sustainable peace and prosperity. The structural disenfranchisement of indigenous communities also prevents them from having any kind of real input regarding the direction of its ongoing conflict resolution process. Lastly, the broader implications of reoccupation for regional stability are extremely difficult to overstate. Solidifying occupation undermines a fragile equilibrium that favours militarism and serves as an incubator for continued struggle and insecurity. This disordering impact can ripple through and increase tensions for collective security throughout the broader region. In summary, the threat of reoccupation casts a shadow over potential conflict resolution, posing significant challenges in the pursuit of peace. Recognising and mitigating these likely outcomes of reoccupation is a key part of mapping a course that will not just provide the real reconciliation, justice, and peace needed by all communities concerned but also empower them.

Pathways to Sustainable Peace

Peacebuilding for sustainable peace in reoccupation is an integral and multilevel process engaging the deep underlying factors of conflict and stability. The strategic channels for sustainable peace in the area will be analysed, taking into account an intricate associational network of political, economic, and sociocultural factors.

Diplomacy and negotiation can result in insufficient, negative, or enduringly positive peace outcomes. Constructive and comprehensive diplomacy are key in ensuring lasting peace. Such cooperation means dialogue with all stakeholders willing to join you and work transparently in finding a joint solution based on mutual respect. Diplomatic avenues should be employed to help foster discussions, forge trust and clear the path for action to target the underlying reasons behind the fighting. The intermediation of international actors can also be decisive in bridging gaps and setting the stage for productive negotiations.

Mechanisms for conflict resolution: Effective mechanisms for conflict redress, ranging from legal systems to institutional apparatuses, are necessary to be able to manage conflicts and prevent escalation. Transparent and equitable grievance resolution procedures, including arbitration, mediation, and judicial processes, help direct disagreements toward peaceful solutions. It is essential to provide a basis for international law and enforce compliance with outside agreements in the interest of stability and further the ethos of upholding the rule of law.

Reconciliation and Renewal: Forgiveness heals the soul, but our memories are what we carry with us. In order to genuinely maintain peace, we must first address past traumas and re-establish connections with those who oppose us. Grassroots organisations, initiatives, and community-based dialogue facilitated healing through truth-seeking and reconciliation processes, paving the way for the pursuit and extension of forgiveness. It is important that the suffering of all affected communities be recognised and addressed as part of an honest reckoning for past injustices to trust each other and share a common vision for peace.

Investment leads to development and prosperity: Addressing socio-economic inequalities and promoting inclusive development are essential components of ongoing peacebuilding efforts. Economic development, employment generation and infrastructure development can be alternatives to progress and well-being that reduce tensions and promote interdependence among various communities. In addition, expanding access to education, healthcare, and essential services can create the basis for a less unjust and vulnerable society.

Culture, Cultural Exchanges, People-to-People Exchanges: It's the people that matter, and operating at this level can narrow gaps and promote mutual understanding. Cultural programs, art exchanges, and educational interactions open hearts, tear down walls of difference, and encourage an understanding of shared humanity. Societies can form connections that will outlive political differences by welcoming diversity and promoting cross-cultural camaraderie.

Security sector reform and confidence-building measures Establishing effective security reforms and confidence-building measures is vital to ensure stability in post-conflict settings. The establishment of credible and professional security institutions, the demilitarisation of disputed territories, and disarmament programs were all critical to creating an environment in which peace could be sustained.

Finally, participating in cooperative security drills and confidence-building measures can improve relations and increase mutual security cooperation between former enemies. Finally, durable peace is contingent upon an integrated approach to all aspects of conflict. The parties can map out a path towards a more peaceful and prosperous future for their region through diplomacy, conflict resolution processes, reconciliation, development cooperation, cultural understanding, and security sector reform.

2
The Crumbling Accords

A Primer on the Accords Framework

The historical background and optimistic expectations for the accords serve as a crucial context for understanding the shortcomings in their implementation. These agreements, designed to promote peace and stability in a region long plagued by hostility and belligerence, embody the dreams and aspirations of generations longing for a peaceful coexistence. Laying down their historical legends, the participants of this agreement agreed to promote friendship and co-operation to work together towards peace and prosperity. The architects carefully laid the foundational blocks of these accords, fostering a spirit of peace and reconciliation, and advocating for respect for sovereignty and dignity on all sides. The accords themselves included the first commitments on a range of scales, social and political as well as economic and security. These adventures were rooted in a shared resolve to set history aside and just do policy in a way that is common between them, like making their own luck with peace and cooperation.

So the accords dawned as a hope that finally forced itself into belief: fit after all for life, peace is possible, and not just life's gasping—nor thenceforward only to shape their destinies. We are presented with the conceptual genealogy and tactical plan for where the frame harbours its profound effects and strikes. A good way to learn more about the process that produced these accords is to recall essential principles at work in this grand experiment. Recognising the hopes and courage hovering over these negotiations as a vision that transcended the current adversity and petrified animosities was beneficial. When we try to make sense of the accords in their historical context, it is the context and early pledges that provide us with our bearings; at this point, we begin to navigate the challenging developments that followed, attempting to determine how we can assess their relevance today.

Historical Context and Initial Promises

The historical background and early initiatives towards the treaties investigate the interaction between a series of developments in geopolitics and diplomacy that eventually resulted in the creation of this pioneering set of principles. The deals come on the back of a heritage of historical resolutions, treaties and UN resolutions to end complex conflicts and bring lasting peace in the region. These early promises reflected an ideal of stability, security and prosperity for all the parties concerned, establishing a condition upon which future events and concessions would depend.

At the beginning of the agreement, there were hopes and a strong belief in reaching a consensus and engaging in peaceful dialogue. The accords were a light of potential, an opportunity to resolve historic grievances and find a path to live together sustainably. At this crucial juncture, pinning aspirational objectives and ambitious visions with bold promises in mutual cooperation was expressed. The international community, with its backing of and mediation between opposing stances, tried to consolidate the arising framework in order to give it as strong a basis of legitimacy and international backing as possible. This historic context, saturated with the spirit of diplomacy and goodwill, laid the ground for addressing historical injustices, making war less painful, as well as creating a conducive atmosphere for confidence-building and reconciliation.

Socio-Political Dynamics and Challenges

A multilayered pattern, reminiscent of an Arabic pattern, intricately weaves the web of socio-political competition that contributed to the destruction of the agreements themselves. Underlying these challenges, however, are entrenched social fractures and political tensions that serve as drivers of violence and have blocked the road to inclusive peace. Deep ethnic, religious and cultural divides have resulted in deep political cleavages with conflicting dreams for the future. What is more, the erosion of trust between all parties has exacerbated these difficulties, and a general mood of mistrust prevails. This atmosphere of hostility has hindered honest and open conversation or peace-mongering, thereby making the body politic still more immovable.

The absence of participatory governance mechanisms and grievance redress structures has further exacerbated these challenges, giving rise to emotions of marginalisation and alienation among specific sections of society. Meanwhile, external influences and geopolitical alliances have put tremendous pressure on the socio-political scene, frequently exacerbating old tensions and issues, with some causing layering over already difficult challenges from within. Strategic alliances, interference by foreign powers, and a tinderbox of regional politics have brought about the collapse of one constructed social shield after another, frustrating the prospects for agreement/consensus on important matters.

The contested nature of history/collective memory and the politicisation of collective memory, therefore, have also been very important in these adjustments. There are divergent views of history, which linger to cause untold tensions and undermine any efforts to achieve a common understanding of what caused the conflicts. That polemicised history has been integrated into the modern sociopolitical discussion and has helped mould contemporary identity formations and the collective imagination of these communities.

Additionally, propaganda and the prevalence of radicalised social and educational media outlets have served only to deepen societal divisions and solidify divides. Asymmetries of information and narratives slanted in opposite directions have prevented the processes that would allow for mutual understanding and empathy – and cycles of hatred and dehumanisation remain.

Addressing these socio-political difficulties necessitates a multifaceted, nuanced response that acknowledges the deeply rooted historical wounds and is attuned to diverse voices, as well as the muddy waters of identity and belonging. Developing inclusive mechanisms for dialogue, enhancing intercultural awareness and promoting participatory decision-making are necessary steps to address these challenges and lay the groundwork for a sustainable peacebuilding routine.

Economic Implications and Expectations

The economic consequences of collapsing accords are also many and far-reaching and should be weighed carefully. The fabric of diplomacy is fraying; economic alliances and trade agreements grow uncertain at best — with a knock-on effect for industries and markets. This lack of stability damages investor confidence, which in turn impedes FDI, which stands to stunt economic growth. In addition, the erosion of political stability caused by the failing accords could lead to fiscal uncertainty and instability in local and regional economies.

Once seen as instruments of future prosperity, the hopes associated with these agreements stand in stark contrast to the new reality, where they are hard-pressed to deliver on their promises in an atmosphere tainted by tensions and bitterness. As commercial links dissolve, countries are forced to seek new roles in world markets, possible future trade alliances and options for diversification that may cushion the blow of losing access to previously strong arrangements.

The same disintegration of international cooperation undermines essential realms like infrastructure building, energy security and durable investment in R&D as both funding and collaboration decline amidst geopolitical ferment. Here, businesses and entrepreneurs are faced with growing pressure to redefine, reinvent, and recalibrate their strategy as the ground shifts beneath them. The undermining of hitherto secure economic alliances requires swift footwork and preemptive steps to protect financial interests and market access.

Whether it's planning for a potential falling apart or exploring new routes for commerce, stakeholders will need to face the unintended consequences of the fraying accords with foresight — and flexibility. In the end, simply put, the economic stakes and prospects for plummeting accords so clearly illustrate that politics and commerce are inexorably intertwined, strengthened by any capacity to face with resilience and strategic foresight whatever perilous ripples may ensue in the wake of political pandemonium.

Security Threats It's a story about security threats and defence tactics

Security and defence matters intrinsically link to the stability and resilience of any agreements in geopolitics. Where the region is concerned, a variety of complicated security dynamics surface and bring different sets of difficulties and complex dilemmas for the stakeholders. Understanding this is crucial if we're to formulate defence policies that are of a strategic and effective nature -- ones ceding threats but nurturing the possibility for enduring peace. This area has a history of conflicts, and so confidence-building and security are hard to come by among the nations. The challenge of negative groupings within and across sovereign states is a persistent threat to regional stability. In addition, the spread of arms and sophisticated weaponry in the region raises the ante and muddies security issues. Defence policies need to take over that traditional military threat perspective – and include the implications of asymmetrical warfare and non-state actors' disregard for established global security processes.

In this turbulent context, avenues for confidence-building measures, trust-building and cooperative security need to be explored. It involves a move away from purely defensive and reactive defence strategies to more active, collaborative approaches. Collective security arrangements designed to mitigate risks and create conflict-management tools can promote a shared responsibility ethos as well as deterrence against potential threats. Alongside, there is a need for strong diplomatic efforts to de-escalate tensions and forge consensus on how to deal with security risks. It is essential to deepen multilateral cooperation and strengthen regional security architecture for a joint response to shared security challenges.

The use of technology and innovation in defence strategies is essential for dealing with changing security threats. Leveraging developments in cyber and intelligence technology, as well as surveillance tools, can improve early-warning systems that pre-empt security breaches. Additionally, regional Maritime Domain Awareness (MDA) through intelligence sharing and combined exercises can help prepare for and respond to developing threats. Factors such as a nationwide policy should also be taken into account in decisions regarding defence. Addressing pre-existing grievances, historical tensions and power imbalances may also go some way toward reducing the underlying sources of insecurity that destabilise the region in general. By realigning defence posture with principled diplomacy, a shared understanding and a common commitment to peaceful coexistence can be waged for sustainable security and lasting peace.

Diplomatic Disputes and Tensions

With the tangled web of geopolitical conflicts surfacing in the vicinity, a common denominator that compounds animosities is diplomatic spats. Often, historic rivalries, people's land and ideological conflicts are involved, which breed long-standing mistrust among parties. Divorce from foreign actors Foreign powers have exacerbated these fights, as a number of world players try to advance strategic goals which often damage the region's stability.

Recognition and legitimacy play a key role in these diplomatic wranglings. Various factions, governments and non-state groups jostle for recognition in the broader world—vying to be noticed and carry their influence outside. This struggle for visibility frequently triggers those clashes and inflames pre-existing tensions so that the diplomatic environment is rarely clear-cut – rather, it is one of conflicting narratives and agendas.

A further cause for the spiral of tension is the collapse of any channels of communication and diplomatic contact. And even when it has tried to hold peace talks or negotiate, mutual mistrust and contradictory motivations make genuine dialogue impossible. As a result, long-festering grievances and misunderstandings remain, while the chances of diplomatic showdowns or even military clashes rise.

Diplomatic missions and envoys figure importantly in this regard. They are intermediaries, seeking to build a bridge across the gorge that divides adversaries and makes conversation impossible. But they are constantly being undermined by hardened positions and agendas, which does not make it easy to reach the great breakthrough in diplomatic paving.

And the role of soft power in terms of diplomacy has also become a matter of growing controversy. Government propaganda, disinformation and proxy wars serve to ratchet up tension by reinforcing hostile mindsets. My purpose here isn't to talk about the line between civil and uncivil behaviour; it's to challenge you to consider how – in this information age, when the battlefield is no longer limited by physical borders but has also flowed into cyberspace – small disputes among diplomats can have an outsized impact.

Consequently, the results of heated rhetoric and diplomatic spats have not only linguistic consequences; instead, they have had dire implications for regional security and relations between states. "Deep discord and growing tensions can only lead to more serious confrontation; the emergency for all of us is to promote dialogue, defuse tensions and avert further escalation."

Voices From the Region: Split Perspectives

The empowering geopolitical relationship in the region has produced numerous viewpoints, which represent a cross-section of opinions between the parties. The conflicting stories and perspectives of local authorities, international agencies, diplomatic communities and grassroots movements reflect the cacophony of opinions that are influencing talks over a floundering deal.

One of the countless general stories here is a recitation of reasons why hatred can't die, why it sustains itself on past grievances and perceived injustices, and further retards whatever momentum remains at hand toward an ultimate solution. This narrative revolves around the historical trajectories of history, territorialisation, and ideology, while also fervently advocating for recognition and restitution.

Conversely, a narrative from the opposing side frequently reiterates the need for practical advancement through economic measures, a shared understanding of security arrangements, and shared interests. Those who hold this view say that the focus should be on getting both sides to stop fearing each other and to believe in their common interests and the ability of joint projects to create trust.

However, within this chorus of conflicting narratives, another layer of dissent emerges from the marginalised voices of refugees, minority communities, and victims of war's aftermath. Their views illustrate the toll of ongoing war, shedding light on social, political, and humanitarian issues underreported in coverage dominated by geopolitics.

Furthermore, regional and international forces will likely complicate matters further with their interests and strategy considerations. Each player will have a unique angle, based on their geopolitical positioning and alliances that it shares, as well as its long-term objectives. These contrasting views highlight issues that are both complex and multifaceted. The various perspectives are interwoven into a patchwork of voices, which present an incredibly valuable synthesis around the complexity of the conflict and a plea to reject simplified understanding by means of dialogue. The tangled web of both-and visions needs to be unwoven, however, by a responsible dialogue that puts some weight on the concerns and hopes (not taking everything as an act) of all parties but also at times finds ways for something to be said that both sides can say at least together while prudently keeping one's mind open. Within this cacophony of voices is the kernel of possibility for resolution, which can frame a comprehensive analysis of forces at work and a potential pathway to sustainable peace.

Case Studies: Analysing Key Failures

In the following, we can identify important counter-examples in this concept wasteland. The purpose of this review of case studies is to uncover insights and implications for managing the complexity and difficulties that lead to the degradation of agreements. By examining in detail some examples of failures of the accords, we can develop a better appreciation for the fundamental and contributory causes for their demise. Every case study will be systematically scrutinised to determine particular information and patterns that showcase these larger narratives of dissonance.

One compelling example is bilateral negotiations between key parties breaking down into intransigency, ossifying long-standing resentment. It is this breakdown, she writes, that shows how incompatible ideologies and strategic goals can be to continued cooperation. In addition, another study will analyse the difficulties of social disparity in unblocking success and how these historical barriers have constituted obstacles for win-win agreements.

Our examination will also cover the security predicaments that are varied and that have dented the success of the accords. Through analysing the dynamics of tension and mistrust build-ups, we can learn about how securing dynamics operates in practice and what implications they have on the durability of agreements. An examination of these case studies from a more critical perspective will help us understand the intricate interplay between historical grudges, political nuances and power dynamics, which in turn can throw some light on the weaknesses of the current accords.

Additionally, a concentrated study of hurdles to diplomacy and recurring disagreements would yield useful data on enduring obstacles that confront accommodation and perpetuate animosity. By closely scrutinising the finer points of diplomatic setbacks and communication failures, we can take from these critical lessons on establishing strong lines of communication and conflict resolution. It is through this close interrogation of the case studies that we hope to elucidate what is lacking in the accords, enabling us to consider broader implications and prospects for recalibrating future agreements.

Implications for Future Agreements

The lessons from peacemaking are invaluable, and history is a harsh teacher. Continued violence in places that were previously peaceful serves as a reminder of the need for genuine understanding of the underlying reasons for conflict and the complicated task of resolving conflicts such that peace endures. As we consider the chain of agreements and treaties that failed in their aims to bring lasting peace, we receive a better view about the complex system of elements leading to these agreements' failure.

More fundamentally, a key lesson of the failed accords

comes into focus upon looking back at them: the need for truly inclusive talks. Permanent peace is only attainable if the parties to the conflict sit around the table and all their concerns, thoughts and desires are heard, discussed and negotiated so that they can be addressed in a final agreement. Inclusivity engenders an ownership and a commitment among the parties which will enhance the possibility of long-term adherence to what is detailed in the agreement.

Secondly, any future agreements also need to recognise that society's dynamics are multi-dimensional and issues are interrelated. Conflicts should not be handled in a simplistic way; it is grossly important to know that political, economic, social and cultural issues interact. If these related aspects are considered holistically, they can help negotiators develop a framework that is better able to deal with the western hopes and tensions. This method allows an agreement to be written that reflects the needs and the wishes of the impacted communities.

A second key lesson is the need for strong verification and enforcement mechanisms in peace agreements. A sustainable peace needs an effective mechanism to monitor compliance and address violations. Including transparent mechanisms that ensure accountability and enforcement of the deal can increase its legitimacy by discouraging others from undermining it.

But also the importance of sustained long-term commitment and investment in post-agreement reconciliation and reconstruction should not be underestimated. 'The peace process is not only a matter of signing papers; it equally carries a moral commitment spanning over time to work on mutual understanding, historical forgiveness and social reconciliation.' There also need to be sufficient resources and psychosocial support for repairing shattered communities, rehabilitating affected populations and reconstituting war-torn infrastructure so that the fabric of peace is integral to society.

Losing from previous mistakes takes the lesson from the necessity of inserting a possibility of dealing with new contingencies and changed realities in future peace treaties. Being flexible and forward-looking in predicting lines of potential conflict is what keeps them from expiring amidst changing geopolitical conditions.

In the end, what has been gleaned from threading the needle of broken agreements are invaluable lessons that help inform strategies for future accords. By learning from them, navigating the intricacies of conflict resolution and nurturing an ethos of inclusiveness, vision and sustained engagement, humanity can help carve paths to peace.

Summary: Paths to a Durable Peace

A holistic approach that includes political, economic, social and security dimensions is required to achieve sustainable peace in the region. Lessons learnt from previous agreements highlight the necessity for comprehensive solutions, tackling the root causes of conflict, and creating a conducive atmosphere for durable peace. It is important to have an open and transparent discussion – it creates the basis for shared understanding and trust between all parties. Building sustainable peace requires ongoing efforts to address grievances, foster inclusive governance, and promote socio-economic development. In addition, investing in education and cultural exchange programs, as well as fostering people-to-people contact, can play a crucial role in breaking down barriers and fostering mutual understanding and cooperation.

The use of technological advances to support improved regional connectivity and greater economic dependence can lead to a mutual interest in peace and prosperity and thus prevent the reemergence of conflict. Security and protection are essential for all concerned, and this can only come with effective preventive, resolutions, and post-conflict reconstruction mechanisms. All of these involve more than just resilient institutions, demilitarised zones, and acceptance culture. Beyond that, international players need to be constructive, supporting regional stakeholders in their efforts while observing and respecting their agency and authority. Strategic alliances and cooperative arrangements to help the process of sustained peace can play a crucial role in sharing resources and knowledge for the well-being of all concerned.

In the end, lasting peace needs a fresh look at traditional ideas so we can use new and flexible methods that fit the changing nature of this region. It demands moving from short-term, transactional diplomacy to sustainable, relationship-based engagement that places the dreams and welfare of all affected people at its core. In conclusion, the realisation of peace may not be a destination but a journey filled with relentless determination, persistence, and innovation. Adopting a shared vision of stability and cooperation, it is possible to imagine that enduring pacification in the region will become achievable – and with it, priceless benefits for future generations.

3
Strategic Encirclement: Turkey and Iran

Introduction to Strategic Encirclement

In geopolitics, strategic encirclement is a political strategy of surrounding an enemy place. It results in stress alleviation and progressive relaxation. This strategy combines a variety of military, diplomatic and economic ways and means to distance criminality that turns the political environment into its own profit. This article explores the multifaceted features of strategic encirclement from its historical origin to its current practice. However, the encirclement strategy ultimately involves playing a complex set of strategic games within a specific regional context, particularly among the major powers in the area, as demonstrated by issues related to proximity, historical ties, and control over resources for national interests.

Throughout history, empires and nation states have used various ways of "encircling" to undermine geopolitical posturing or promote regime change / deter threats. The rediscovery of Ottoman pretensions and the renewal of Iranian ambitions are essential components in this narrative. The powerful legacy of the Ottoman Empire reverberates throughout the Middle East to this day, informing contemporary alliances and divisions.

Meanwhile, Iran's rise as a regional power upsets a traditional balance of power, leading to a nebulous and conflict-ridden arena of reconfigured alliances. Moreover, modern strategic encirclement is not limited to the military form of containment that has historical precedent and incorporates all types of instruments, from information warfare and cyberattacks to economic agreements, which underlines how power projection is changing. Both state and non-state actors apply ever more subtle methods that challenge the distinctions between overt force and covert subversion.

It is in this first context that strategic encirclement becomes a basic concept for reading the delle contingenze geopolitiche seconda organic relations of forces determining this part of the world lying between Africa and Central Asia. It provides a framing in terms of historical precedents and current power relations that helps both situate and enrich the analysis it offers in subsequent chapters. If we can view this in different disciplinary ways, perhaps we will gain some insight into how, through multiple mechanisms, circumstances come together in strategic engulfment to think about its broader consequences.

Historical Context: Ottoman Echoes and Iranian Revival

The strategic encirclement with Turkey and Iran has historical underpinnings on the one hand in the decline of the Ottoman Empire as far as Erdoğan is concerned and on the other hand for post-revolutionary Iran. The legacy of these predecessors still plays an important role in the geopolitical system of the Middle East and influences alliances, enmities and aspirations toward regional hegemony.

With its 14th-century establishment, the Ottoman Empire not only became a regional superpower but also left its mark on contemporary Turkish national identity and foreign policy. Its far-reaching territorial aspirations, as well as the model of power projection it embodied, are relevant in the contexts of Turkey's current foreign policy initiatives toward regaining influence over territories that once fell within its sphere. Concurrently, the revival of Iran as a sovereign regional actor frames present encirclement policies. The deep historical pattern of civilisation and empire in Iran underpins what is happening now, with its centuries-old ambition to exercise hegemony and command.

The turning point came in 1979 with the Islamic Revolution, and Iran established itself as a revolutionary entity; it became effectively ground zero for anti-establishment forces throughout the region. Such a history is a prerequisite in order to understand the current political contest between Turkey and Iran, as each of these has sought to revive an imperial past in pursuit of its regional interests. Those of us living in the modern world with 'geopolitically smart' instincts cannot escape learning and knowing history. It explains the motivations, interests, and grievances that are behind Turkey's and Iran's conduct in their interactions and strategic calculations. These are only a few of the complex pieces that comprise the geophysical mosaic of today's Middle East, with its remnants of Ottoman rule and resurgence in Iranian power.

Geopolitical Dynamics: Shifting Alliances

A dense kaleidoscope of ever-turning alliances between rival regional players has been a hallmark of Middle Eastern politics for some time now. Old rivalries, border animosities, and geopolitical aspirations all clamour for dominance across the region's complex strategic topography. Those shifting coalitions sometimes also shed light on global power politics generally and some geopolitical reconfiguration more broadly. Other factors such as religion, ethnicity, and ideology enhance the fluidity of these partnerships.

A variety of internal and external factors constantly shift the Middle East's tectonics. Fluctuations in energy markets, the fortunes of empires, and the resolution of transnational conflicts are just a few external drivers that impact this situation. Internally, political turmoil and popular unrest, as well as ambitions, also matter. Amidst this labyrinth of interests, the policies and behaviours of the regional powers, like Turkey or Iran, contribute decisively to geopolitics. Their dealings with other regional players, as well as their relationships with international powers, are also a major influence in the balance of power there. The constant shifting of alliances and affiliations redefines the global balance, favouring optimal winners and losers. Understanding these changing dynamics is critical when seeking to comprehend the delicate balance of power in the region, as well as develop policies that can best contribute to regional stability and conflict resolution.

Turkey's Strategic Ambitions in the Middle East

Turkey, once the symbol of an empire and the crucible of mankind's civilisation, is a country with a history as rich and colourful as its people! It is a key player in the region due to its geographic location that connects Europe and Asia. Turkish Perspective Mesut Casin To regain its regional position, Turkey has implemented a multidimensional fight-or-flight approach designed for underlining its position as a key international player. Central to Turkey's strategic aspirations is the desire to maintain and grow its control over the Middle East. Turkey seeks to project economic, political, and military power in the region on the basis of shared cultures and histories with its neighbours, further enhancing its status as a key actor in regional development.

Under President Recep Tayyip Erdoğan, Turkey has pursued a foreign policy of coercive pragmatism in pursuit of its long-held ambition to become more active in regional affairs. This is in line with Turkey's historical policies of building relations with its neighbours, as portrayed through key issues, such as the Syrian crisis and energy disputes in the Mediterranean. In addition, Turkey uses soft power mechanisms, such as cultural diplomacy, humanitarian assistance, and public diplomacy campaigns, to enhance its influence and create positive perceptions in the region.

In addition, Ankara is concentrating on infrastructure projects, including the planned Istanbul Canal, as well as investments demanded by crucial sectors like energy, thus emerging as a major provider for connectivity and regional integration. However, these lofty ambitions are accompanied by a plethora of formidable challenges that Turkey must overcome. These challenges range from diplomatic entanglements and chaos in regional and international relations, to internal security issues and unfriendly meddling in its affairs by regional and global actors vying for influence in the Middle East. The delicate balance Turkey must maintain between collaborating with and competing with Iran, Saudi Arabia, and Israel intensifies the complexity of the situation, requiring Ankara to navigate a perilous geopolitical path as regional geopolitics 'evolve'. In navigating the murky landscape of Middle Eastern politics, Turkey seeks to expand its historic pan-Islamism into broader strategic interests. One starting point that moves beyond the knowledge gap is an understanding of the intersection between historical aspirations and current policies and future ambitions to dominate the region.

Iran's Expanding Influence: Beyond Proxy Wars

Iran's growing centrality as a key regional player goes beyond proxy struggles and regional dynamics. The Islamic Republic's influence extends beyond its borders into the complex political, social, economic, and security terrains that surprisingly define this region. There are many inducements that lie behind Iran's strategic thrust, including military intervention, economic cooperation, ideological exports, and diplomatic manipulation. On the battlefield, Iran's influence reaches deep into the Middle East, thanks to networks of clients—sometimes called proxies—that give Tehran its stamp in Iraq, Syria, and Lebanon. This approach to asymmetric warfare allows Iran to exert power and influence in neighbouring countries, influencing conflicts and political results.

Additionally, Iran's development of ballistic missile technologies and advanced weapons demonstrates a desire to increase regional influence and optimise deterrence. Politically, Iran has extended its trade ties, held elected office in the government and developed relations on transnational bases with a wide variety of countries across the Middle East that serve to increase influence as well as allow for strong interdependence. Iran, which has large energy resources and financial reasons for acting overtly in the regional power balance, is attempting to stake as powerful a claim as possible on that regional economic future so that regional calculations will go in Tehran's favour.

Iran has established itself as a practical ideological hegemon in the Middle East and Muslims more generally, projecting its version of revolutionary Shiism and deep opposition to "Western imperialism". This story also plays well to anti-western sentiments that are abundant in the region, helping Iran form alliances and ideological affinities that cut across traditional nation-state borders—and thus its influence and soft power.

On the diplomatic front, Iran uses a multipronged and flexible approach that spans multilateralism and bilateralism while making forays to create coalitions in an attempt to manage regional and international dimensions. Iran's diplomatic initiatives aim to forge alliances that counter common enemies while also maintaining support for a domestic regional axis and addressing outrage abroad, which reflects its aspiration to extend beyond the regional context. Therefore, one cannot fully comprehend Iran's influence by relying solely on conventional realist geopolitical and military perspectives, as it involves not just one-dimensional state power but rather a combination of hard and soft elements, including military capabilities, economic capacity building, and ideological narrative strategies that together form an integrated approach to establishing regional hegemony.

The Intersection of Energy Politics

The value of Middle Eastern oil transcends economic factors: it has complex security, strategic and diplomatic dimensions. For decades, natural resources such as oil and gas dictated regional power relations across the Middle East -- determining everything from alliances and conflicts to foreign policies. With global energy needs still growing, the Middle East is a vital source of supply— and power plays. Countries use these resources to exert influence both on the global stage and internally.

Recent power competition for new energy sources and transport routes has also sharpened local rivalries between the key regional actors, with their alliances and hostilities forming a complex tapestry of cooperation and conflict that defines the marshy mix. The impact of energy politics on interstate relations is significant, as countries experience both rapprochement or détente due to shared agendas and disappointment stemming from their increasingly divergent trajectories.

What's more, the quest for energy security has led to heavy investment in military assets and infrastructure by nations that militarise their energy supply chains and insecure production areas. This hybridisation of the security and energy supply spheres leads to a situation in which both entities heavily affect one another. Territorial disputes, pipeline routes, and access to maritime chokepoints may characterise debates on energy geopolitics as contentious arenas, but they also reveal more strategic complications specific to each country.

States aim to protect their economic interests and mitigate threats to their energy infrastructures posed by other nations, with the relationship between energy politics and regional security structures serving as the crucial point around which the balance of power revolves. The changing terrain of hybrid warfare, which uses irregular methods for energy purposes, also highlights the link between security and energy. Moreover, rising concerns about the environment and the demand for clean energy sources have introduced more challenges to the politics of energy production and distribution. The fact that the region is moving in the direction of renewable energy and adopting it as a way forward for future energy needs signals that it is stepping into new political territory, one that will define its character for the next few decades.

The Case of Military Posture and Defence Strategies

Major regional players have always dominated the Middle East, from its military appearance to its defensive approach. With the escalation and mixing of rival conflicts within the region in recent years, military capacities used have become more and more a means of leverage and power projection. While countries like Turkey and Iran are looking to build up their military capabilities, it isn't so much for sovereignty or security as power projection – be it to gain access to strategic resources on their own terms or an acceptance of regional geopolitics that benefits from their meddling. This is a military movement with far-reaching implications for international relations.

A NATO member, Turkey is no prudent hardliner; its military knows no boundaries. The military and the military base of Turkey, one of the great air–land powers of the world and easily dominating the Eastern Mediterranean in terms of firepower, are operating outside its national territory. Turkey's participation in various conflicts ranging from Syria to Iraq shows the strategic location of the country straddling Europe and Asia that dominates important sea trade and energy routes. Turkey is a major military force in its region and beyond.

On the other hand, Iran's defence policies are based on post-revolutionary experiences and its need to preserve the national identity. Iran has invested heavily in its military, developing new products such as missiles and advanced radar systems. The IRGC is instrumental in protecting the regime's interest, and it furthers its reach by means like using proxy forces and guerrilla campaigns. Both Turkey and Iran, understanding the new structures of regional competition and security threats, have built alliances and proxies to advance their geopolitical goals.

The dynamic interaction between diplomacy and force posturing is such a complex process that the structure of regional dynamics itself becomes a generative factor, increasing the risk of escalation at multiple levels. The Turkish and Iranian expansion into the neighbouring countries upsets attempts for peace, whilst local alignments of forces frustrate local stability ambitions. This is symptomatic of how modern-day geopolitics work on two levels, because it demonstrates how symmetric and asymmetric threats are intricately bound together; the orders of battle (justified or not) will continue to serve as a decisive factor in shaping regional balance over the trend period.

If one seeks to understand the changing character of armed forces in contemporary society, one must analyse the nature of power and influence. There is a need for an understanding of how these elements synergise in a landscape that would be condoned by the authorities who maintain the status quo and has been espoused by many across Asia, as well as from among peers in Europe and North America.

Diplomatic Manoeuvres and Regional Implications

Diplomatic moves are instrumental for the definition of the political geography in the Middle East; in particular, this is true within the intertwined network of strategic encirclements that target Turkey and Iran. Relations, alliances, rivalries, and negotiations among states have a critical impact on regional stability and security, with echoes in global dynamics. This chapter focuses on the consequences of diplomatic games played in the context of strategic encirclement.

At their centre, these diplomatic initiatives reflect the strategic linking of national interests and nationalist aspirations with larger geopolitical currents. Turkey and Iran serve as key players in the Eurasian Chess Game. Turkey and Iran, major protagonists in this geostrategic game of chess, use different diplomatic tools to improve their positioning and influence in the region. These diplomatic channels are conduits for exerting influence on the world stage and promoting domestic policies, as well as ways to control and manage relations between the two countries at a more superficial level.

The intricacies of the diplomatic ballet go beyond political interactions at the state level and involve a wide range of non-state actors, transnational organisations, and external parties with respective stakes in the region. In this dynamic context, we have the "grey zone of strategic encirclement," where alliances are formed and broken, partnerships redefined, and conflicts resolved or escalated according to future requirements.

These diplomatic plays impact the region in economic, security, and ideological dimensions. Trade-based cooperative accords and economic and energy integration because of diplomatic outreach also exert themselves in the region by promoting perceptions of prosperity or decline. At the same time, security agreements and military alliances are not demonstrative of actual power balances to be used during a crisis but rather structural reactions to diplomatic initiatives, which can further endanger regional stability.

In ideological respect, diplomatic activities generate stages for promoting soft power, carrying out cultural exchanges and making ideological alignments. As a result, axes of influence take form counter to each other on the world map, thus creating multiple rifts and imbrications that determine geopolitical paths. This ideological subtext runs through all attempts at diplomacy, subtly affecting the nature of sociopolitical discourse in the region and elsewhere.

In summary, a balanced perspective is necessary to interpret the constantly shifting geopolitical landscapes on both sides of this diplomatic manoeuvre, which unfolds under the shadow of strategic encirclement. This rich and varied pattern of diplomacy reflects the crucial importance of that art in determining nation-states' destinies and, therefore, world events.

Case Studies: Key Incidents and Their Impacts

To look at the nuances of Turkish and Iranian behaviors and their implications, we need cases. Here, one can understand a case study as an in-depth analysis of particular events or situations to include broader patterns. An example worth noting is Syria, where Turkish and Iranian interests coincide. Turkey's support for certain opposition forces and its invasion of northern Syria have disrupted a long-standing balance of power, resulting in a network of conflicts that are both complex and fragmented. Iran's unwavering support for the Assad government, and its dispatch of a plethora of Iran-backed militias has only served to extend the war while bolstering Iran's power in the Middle East. This specific PET case illustrates the complexity of Turkish-Iranian relations and their interventions in Syria, particularly regarding their respective roles.

The Kurdish question emerges as another significant issue, especially given how Turkey and Iran either assist or obstruct each other. The dreams of self-government pursued by these competing Kurdish factions stir up different attitudes from Iran and Turkey, resulting in complex negotiations across the frontlines, which are punctuated with battlefield skirmishes as well as rounds of diplomacy at village bazaars nearby. The dispute is a global problem that goes beyond one country, it overtakes the whole Middle East, and affects regional security. By comparison, considering Turkish military incursions into northern Iraq in the context of Iran's growing influence within Iraqi politics offers insight into both states' motives and tactics, the latter's success or failure with respect to these actions.

These cases shed light on the crucial role of Turkey and Iran in shaping regional developments, and underscore the linkage between their actions, which has significant implications. The analysis of these critical events reveals that the balance between Turkey and Iran continues to determine Middle East stability. Hence, it is of utmost importance to comprehend these cases and come up with a collaborative solution aimed at reducing tensions and reviving normalcy over time.

Conclusion: From Tension to Resolution

THE CRISIS As historical grievances, localised tensions, and a tangled web of relations between nation states come to convergence, we stand at a crossroads where solutions are possible. The presentations in this book shed light on the outcomes of the long-suffering rivalry between Turkey and Iran, bringing out a picture of the balance of power in a region moulded by more than just political aspirations but also regional tussles for hegemony. If anything, the story of conflict falls far short of capturing a potential narrative of reconciliation and transformative diplomacy. In negotiating the complex strata of rivalry and enmity, it is clear that the road to settlement must be less conventional and more innovative.

Turkey and Iran have limited choices that will decide their fates; these choices compel them to carefully question whether to continue their current hostility or reorient towards coexistence. Appreciating their common past, cultural affinity, and economic interdependence can promote a better understanding between them. Diplomacy, if it is inclusive, is the basis for cooperation that endures. We should not underestimate the contribution of external players who successfully engaged the parties in dialogue and mediation. When necessary, the international community can use its diplomatic acumen and strategic might to provide meaningful inducements and balance against elements that inflame discord.

If the parties can overcome a zero-sum mentality to pursue cooperation, they can build a new way that places more emphasis on collective growth and stability at home over just national interest. The new energy landscape in the Middle East offers an unprecedented opportunity for cross-border ventures that overcome historical rivalries. Energy collaboration and healthy infrastructure can be peace bridges. With a little imagination, even regional politics could be reconceptualised as responses to the factors underlying economic development if they were accompanied by approaches directed towards peace. Overall, the issue revolves around leadership and sustained engagement, which requires a commitment to resolution while ignoring provocations and avoiding nit-picking at history. It calls for bravely moving away from face-to-face tough stand-offs to open dialogue, with a focus on rebuilding trust and sharing common aspirations. That's the question as we navigate these fraught relations between Turkey and Iran. In the end, and with dedication and wisdom, hostility can turn to mutual good, and former enemies become partners.

4
The Target is the Gulf

The Gulf as a Strategic Factor in History

The history of the strategic importance of the Gulf over the years and decades is a story of geopolitical manoeuvres, trade routes and changing power balances. Throughout times past, the Gulf has been an important hub for trade, being able to take goods from East to West and vice versa thanks to its connection with the Indian Ocean and beyond. The strategic geopolitical position of the area dates back to ancient times with the important pass-like corridors that connect the commerce and culture diversities in Asian land: the Iranian Plateau. Over the centuries, the Gulf became an important crossroads of global commerce and competition, drawing the interest of empires from Persia to the Ottomans as they vied for control over its rich networks and ports.

Portuguese and other European powers found interest in the region from the 16th century, when they recognised the opportunity to monopolise trade in the Persian Gulf and Arab Sea. The discovery of huge oil deposits in the Gulf in the 20th century propelled it into a central focus of global geopolitics. The sudden wash of oil turned the Gulf states into major power brokers of the world energy market and forged alliances and enmities that still echo.

The Cold War also made the Gulf more strategic, as both superpowers were eyeing it in vying to gain presence and influence there. The Gulf was a theatre of war in the battle for ideological dominance, which manifested in both conventional and covert military interventions, as well as a recasting of regional alliances. The post–Cold War period of the early 1990s did not reduce Asia's strategic salience but instead brought to the fore new content and challenges associated with major powers recalibrating their engagement to manage new threats and opportunities in a post-Cold War order.

The Gulf continues to be a keystone in international relations; it goes beyond simply energy resources and includes maritime security, regional security and the balance of power globally. History of the Gulf's Strategic Significance Of all the regions in the world today, almost certainly none was more intimately interconnected with its wider surrounds than the Gulf. 16 Appreciating this historical significance i s, therefore, fundamental for discerning complex causes that shape and influence developments across it and inform contemporary decisions on how to manage changes within its complex geopolitical environment

Political Alliances and Their Evolution

Political allies in the Gulf have been key to cementing its modern geopolitics. Such partnerships are traditionally built on common security threats, economic interests, and cultural values. The history of these alliances dates to the pre-oil age, when tribal federations and seaborne trade routes formed the basis for regional collaboration. But the oil discoveries of the 20th century changed Gulf political alliances as global powers competed for access to the region's resource. During the Cold War, competition in the region's strategic value saw overlapping patterns of alliances and enmities. Throughout this time, the United States and the

Soviet Union vied for military bases and diplomatic advantage, leading Gulf countries to side with one superpower or the other.

The end of the Cold War was accompanied by a realignment of forces, as non-state actors and private companies followed suit to exploit economic opportunities in the region. In addition, the 21st century has ushered in a new era of geopolitics led by the ascent of Asian economies and greater interdependence among world markets. This has in turn prompted states in the Gulf to hedge their alliances with non-Western major powers, forming strategic partnerships with China, India and Russia, among others. The shifting of alliances is affected partly by internal power struggles, sectarian tensions and the broader regional competition for dominance. Central to this is the ability of Gulf states to negotiate these competing dynamics and how they balance power while managing the unstable environment. Additionally, the nexus between alliances and ideological currents like pan-Arabism as well as political Islam compounds the complexities of shifting geopolitics. So in summary, the impetus and development of political alliances is a terrain rich with opportunities to understand the complex web of desires, connections, and hopes that characterise the Gulf's engagement with the world.

Economic Interests: Oil and Beyond

The Gulf is synonymous with oil, and it provides the world's energy market a foundation for its operation. But this economic powerhouse conceals under it multiple varied objectives that transcend purely extracting resources. Oil, along with gas, is the lifeblood of local economies in the region, which shares borders with several conflict-torn Arabian Peninsula states and where industrialisation and infrastructure investment are key to development. The central importance of oil in politics should not obscure the power wielded by the Gulf states as a whole, thanks to their energy exports. These states have also diversified their economies, starting f rom the finance and technology sectors to tourism and re newable energies for a sustainable and resilient recovery.

The Gulf, adopting its own futuristic tinctured vision, has used its economic weight to encourage innovation, entrepreneurship and knowledge-based industries. This transition to a more diversified economy is consistent with the d esire to decrease its reliance on hydrocarbon revenues, p romote job creation and develop a healthy private sector. In addition to the traditional economic sector, a second part of this broader vision that Gulf states are pursuing is moving beyond their core geography by becoming trade logistics and financial hubs, exploiting their strategic location. Projects such as free zones and special economic clusters are j ust a few of the examples that epitomise the dedication they mix to stimulating an enabling business environment, encouraging FDI (foreign direct investment) and promoting innovation. In addition, the area's sovereign wealth funds have become major players in global investment, spreading their bets across asset types and jurisdictions. These investments are financially profitable but also facilitate the tr ansfer of knowledge, technology, and good practice.

Next, the Gulf's economic interests are not bound by a traditional definition and now also include sustainability, c limate action and social good. It is a once-in-a-lifetime o pportunity to determine the future of the region, with new industries in areas like clean energy, smart infrastructure and digital transformation changing some old assumptions. Using their economies as a power base, the Gulf states are implementing ambitious programmes to tackle environmental issues, advance sustainability and foster social well-being. With such diversification of economic interests, including a way from oil, Gulf societies are strengthening their resilience, opening themselves up to the global network of interactions and asserting themselves as active elements in a world that is transforming.

Military Presence and Implications

The military presence in the Gulf has been a hot topic in geopolitics for several decades, with wider implications for the stability of the GCC and global security. The Gulf is easily militarily knocked into shape sufficiently deep to obey because of the weight of regional and international military forces in its waters. And the United States still has an extensive military presence in the form of naval fleets, airbases and whatnot across the Gulf states, where it stands as a symbol of security, which has some sort of definite guarantee for confronting threats from outside. Furthermore, the Gulf states have increased their military capacities through massive arms purchases, joint military manoeuvres and defence cooperation pacts with big powers. This military build-up has thinned out the regional balance of power, besides promoting fears about arms proliferation, destabilising wars and arms races across the Gulf region.

Dynamics of conflict and security are fluid.

The dynamics of warfare on the Arabian Peninsula – or here, the Persian Gulf – have changed tremendously due to the presence of more militarised zones and advances in military technology. This has been compounded by the development and deployment of missile defence systems, next-generation fighter aircraft and unmanned aerial vehicles (UAVs) that have added new layers to deterrence and defence strategies as well as increased capabilities for state and non-state actors to project power in the region. The military posture in the Gulf also has broader implications for global energy security, with the passage of oil and natural gas through the strategic Strait of Hormuz critical to the global economy. Such an accident could further inflame tensions and conflicts in the Gulf, potentially undermining energy supplies to markets around the world with repercussions for the global economy while reinforcing a strategic imperative for protection of regional maritime trade routes and key installations.

In addition to conventional military assets, growing cyber and space-based needs have added a new dimension to security issues in the Gulf. Security risks have also been extended due to the exposure of vital infrastructures and information systems to cyber threats, in addition to the increasing militarisation of space, which entails that a comprehensive strategy is required for protecting national and regional interests. The nexus of military footprint, diplomatic ties and economic stakes in the Gulf highlights complex geopolitical chess games determining the course of this region. In a constantly changing strategic equation, it is important to have a comprehensive understanding of the dynamics at play in military deployments in the Gulf and to encourage discussions that can lead towards security frameworks capable of ensuring sustainability.

Influence of Non-State Actors

Influencing non-state actors has also featured prominently in establishing the dynamics of the Gulf as a factor within geopolitical, economic, and security dimensions. Ranging from transnational terrorist networks to proxy militias supported by regional powers, these groups have woven a complex web of interrelated conflicts coursing through the Gulf. Perhaps the most prominent non-state actor is Hezbollah, a Shia militant organisation based in Lebanon which has strong links to Iran. Hezbollah's intervention in the Syrian war and backing of Houthi insurgents have contributed to further tensions in the region and deepened sectarian rifts.

Moreover, power vacuums and sectarian grievances have been the causative factors for non-state actors, including Al-Qaeda and ISIS (Daesh), to operate against others, which resulted in destabilisation and violence. The influence of these non-state actors is not only confined to the region but also contributes to international security challenges associated with terror and the trend in radicalisation. Moreover, the cyber warfare capabilities of non-state actors worldwide are an increasing threat, in which organisations carry out advanced cyber attacks to damage essential infrastructure's integrity, breach confidential data and even conduct information warfare. This changing aspect of non-state actor influence requires proactive measures to address Gulf cybersecurity threats.

Non-state players have also played a big role in drawing and reshaping the Gulf's economy, mostly via illegal transactions like weapons smuggling or money laundering or extortion. Such activities destabilise the country and compound existing issues of governance and state capacity. The contribution of non-state actors in economic realms further complicates the process of achieving development and prosperity in the region. Therefore, to neutralise the influence of these non-state actors, a multi-dimensional approach is required which involves strong security cooperation, intelligence sharing, counter-terrorism and enhancing cyber defence. Acknowledging the connection between these challenges is necessary to respond effectively and neutralise the influence of non-state actors in the GCC area.

Cybersecurity Threats in the Gulf Region

With each passing day, the Gulf region is investing more and more in digitally enabled technologies, infrastructure, and amenities, leading to increased worry about potential security risks. As the use of modern information technology becomes more widespread in all sectors and functions of the government, the risks posed by cyber attacks on the technology that underpins the various vital services provided by the government increase. The deep interdisciplinary and infrastructural ties that Gulf countries have make the possible ramifications of cybersecurity incidents more severe, which warrants geopolitical focus.

The Gulf countries face cybersecurity issues that span the entire spectrum of the phenomenon and continue to evolve, including state-sponsored cyber espionage, cyber ransomware and hacking, as well as other non-cognisant malicious attacks. Besides the physical safety and traditional military efforts of the Gulf countries, the new cybersecurity challenges from the online world are complicated and cover a lot of ground. The existence of sophisticated cyberwarfare tactics in Gulf countries also emphasises the importance of a balanced cyberdefence initiative that includes both active and passive elements. Given the complexities of the situation, the Gulf Cooperation Council countries are of particular importance. The Gulf Cooperation Council member countries require sophisticated cybersecurity technologies, specialised and experienced military personnel, and a modicum of coordinated efforts to face the emerging cyber defence challenges and threats in a cohesive and multi-dimensional manner.

Additionally, the enhancement of awareness, along with the improvement of competency programmes, can equip organisations as well as individuals to identify and handle possible cyber threats with greater efficiency. The growth o f digital ecosystems, in addition to the growth of intelligent d evices, increases the need for flexible, adaptable, and quick c ontrol of the regulations to protect sensitive and critical inf- ormation. The Gulf region is undergoing rapid technological d evelopment, and with it, the escalating need for the control o f cyber threats. By recognising the multi-domain nature of c yber threats, Gulf countries can navigate the complex digital w orld with confidence and determination.

Soft Power Diplomacy: A Double-Edged Sword

Soft power diplomacy, a term coined by political scientist Joseph Nye, has become a crucial element of influence in international relations. It is founded on the power of attraction and the ability to persuade without coercing, especially through culture. In the Gulf region, however, the use of soft power has become a double-edged sword, as influential actors attempt to use it to consolidate and extend their geo-economic influence. The ability of Gulf states to enhance their image through expensive and prestigious soft power tools, like top global universities, well-known media companies, famous museums, and costly international sports events, shows how these Gulf autocracies are trying to promote a modern image and connect with elite global citizens. These autocracies seek to improve global perceptions of these Gulf autocracies in order to address the global public relations efforts of these autocracies. These Gulf autocracies seek to address their global public relations soft power stereotypes, garner elite global soft power citizenship, and justify international relationships based on soft power interests.

These Gulf soft power autocracies face the soft power paradox of their stereotypes. One of the central paradoxes of the Gulf soft power stereotypes is the invisibility of the soft power of the autocracies in the promotion of the invisibility of human rights and the promotion of social freedom. Social autocracies often use soft power to create the perception of social order and the suppression of social dissent. This social order and social dissent paradox is global. The promotion of social order through the permanent suppression of dissent paradox is global. The global invisibility of the narratives presented to justify soft power erodes the central purpose of soft power. Additionally, the soft power paradox is the creation of social order through social relationships and social contracts to promote social order. The social order paradox has the potential to erode social order through the social relationships and social contracts to promote social order. The social order paradox has the potential to erode the social order through the social and political contracts of social order. The social order paradox has the potential to be perceived as social colonisation and to be devoid of social order. The social order paradox is relational social order and basic democracy.

Thus, the complex nature of international relations soft power utilises has led to international political contention for the advancement of diplomatic relationships to negatively utilise soft power in global politics. As global politics has shifted, the use of soft power in diplomacy in the Gulf has negatively impacted spheres of international politics. Cultural relations, international exchanges, and diplomacy have rivalled cross-country soft power. The Gulf has become a world focus, shifting international relations power to the use of soft power. The consequences of the interaction of soft power and diplomacy require a relationship with the primary flaw of cultural and historical political control. The parameters of world political control will require the interaction of soft power to change with positive world democratic ideals. More specifically, the interaction of soft power will r equire the ideals of positive global democracy to change w orld political control.

The Impact of Multilateral Institutions

The Gulf region maintains a complex balance of multilateral political relationships that involve intricate dynamics of politics, economics, and security. Multilateral institutions create a framework for diplomacy, politics, and economics.

An example includes the Gulf Cooperation Council (GCC), which has mainly contributed to the integration and cooperation of the member states in trade, security, and culture. The efforts of the GCC in managing the region's challenges and fostering the diversification of economic activities have had a significant impact on shaping the identity and aspirations of the Gulf states. In addition to the GCC, the Gulf Region has been the target of several multilateral organisations, such as the United Nations and the Arab League. These multilateral organisations serve as points of engagement and mediation by providing conflict resolution and establishing frameworks for addressing transnational issues in the region, as well as promoting international law and justice. To a great extent, their initiatives in humanitarian actions and the provision of development assistance highlight the importance of multilateral cooperation in the region. However, the impact of multilateral organisations in the Gulf is complex and presents several challenges. The need for diplomacy and consensus-building in these organisations is crucial in dealing with the challenges posed by different national agendas, historical conflicts, and geopolitics.

Furthermore, instances of external interference, control imbalances, and organisational boundaries affect the effectiveness of multilateral collaboration. Therefore, a more granular approach to multilateral cooperation requires Gulf states to consider these issues carefully. Therefore, the Gulf states need to prioritise their national stances and overarching plans when participating in these multilateral institutions. The functions of multilateral institutions in the Gulf have been, and continue to be, the promotion of cross-border activities, the establishment of interregional norms, and the provision of diplomatic services to facilitate the management of interstate relations in the Gulf. These institutions promote and manage dialogue and cooperation. These institutions are a testimony to the modern realities of global governance and the need for cooperation to respond to global issues. These institutions reflect the modern realities of global governance and the need for cooperation to respond to global issues. Multilateral organisations must adapt to the complex and rapidly evolving geopolitical environment that the Gulf continues to face. Hence, the institutions will continue to be of great importance in attaining a coordinated approach to the complex geopolitical environment of the Gulf, sustainable development, and security for all the actors there.

Internal Dynamics: Monarchies and modernisation

Monarchies in the Gulf have long been a central part of the political structure, with their idiosyncratic configurations d etermining how states modernise. The conventional configurations of power and authority within the monarchies ha ve changed substantially and will continue to transform in response to the modernisation efforts that are aimed at ec onomic diversification, social development, and political reform in the states.

These initiatives require balancing cultural preservation with global adaptation. Monarchs are also instrumental in the implementation of reforms and are frequently empowered to advocate structural changes because of their position in the hierarchy, which is often complicated by their tribal and familial allegiances. The 'joint venture' between rulers and the ruled has established the framework for political relations in these units, and as a result, rulers are expected to promote both traditional and modern practices.

Furthermore, to respond to the inclusive-development challenges, which also have a focus on fostering social cohesion, these political units have responded to the population development challenges through education, health, and employment, which, to an extent, has been a departure from social orthodoxies, although it has been in line with the needs of an emerging population. The focus on development has also brought a positive change in these units' economies, as there is an increased emphasis on development initiatives which are aimed at diversifying economies which have been oil-dependent. The aims and objectives of the development initiatives to create a knowledge-based economy, promote and sustain a culture of entrepreneurship, and improve foreign direct investment to the units have increased the global position of the region. The positive changes also influenced the governance of the units, which required a change of governance of the units in the region. The units have faced significant challenges in navigating the interface between modernisation and monarchy.

The introduction of major changes has led to significant progress and success, but it has also sparked debates about p rotecting cultural identity, the role of religious leaders, and the balance of power. The merging of power and difficulties of succession have complicated the internal mechanisms in these monarchies, requiring the ruling elites to exercise precisely their internal control. In years to come, a mix of internal and external factors will continue to determine the trajectory of modernisation in the Gulf monarchies. How well these states balance modernisation with their cultural traditions will greatly influence their goals for sustainable development, regional power, and deeper involvement in the global economy, and the connections they build both inside and outside the Gulf will affect how modernisation and the Gulf monarchies come together.

Future Trajectories: Challenges and Opportunities

The anticipated future of the Gulf Region will present a combination of opportunities and challenges. The Gulf monarchies will need to grapple with a number of internal and external factors, and in the new global geopolitical environment, one of the main challenges will be how to integrate modern socio-economic development and diversification into the traditional monarchical structures.

Consequently, balancing the preservation of traditions and the adoption of novelties, including managing the public face of acceleration, becomes particularly important. Forecasting the Gulf's future is further complicated by its strategic location, which is surrounded by geopolitical rivalries and unstable regional security and allegiances. Ongoing problems and power struggles in the Global South, especially in the Middle

East, create challenges for supply and control, increasing the need for modern diplomacy and business innovation in the Gulf countries.

Despite the challenges, the rapid integration of the global economy and the modern technological wave, along with the active crises in the Global South, provide the Gulf countries with a high-growth, socio-economically transformed global economy based on diversification and advanced knowledge. Opening up to a green economy based on energy transition, the development of innovation ecosystems and the active investment in education and training, the Gulf Countries can easily position themselves as leaders in the green economy and technological innovation. The Gulf countries have already rebased global inter-economic relations by adjusting commodity trade. The Gulf can easily position itself in its global inter-economic relations by adjusting the commodity trade. The Gulf can easily position itself in its economy; strategically trading with the Gulf countries has already rebased global inter-economic relations by adjusting commodities trade. The Gulf can easily position itself in its economy. The Gulf Countries have already rebased global inter-economic relations by adjusting commodities trade, and more is still to come.

Because of their unique geography and valuable resources, the Gulf monarchies can form influential connections and gain prominence within the global market. The future paths of the Gulf monarchies will involve the intertwined historical challenges, current circumstances, and potential opportunities of the region. These developments will require strategic planning, flexible control, and the ability to utilise the region's inner potential while building the necessary self-sufficiency to withstand external forces.

5
Geopolitics of the 'Greater Israel'

Historical Underpinnings of the 'Greater Israel' Concept

The idea of "Greater Israel" can trace its beginnings to the early Zionist movement that was on the rise toward the end of the 19th century. The ideology of Zionism was built on the desire of the Jewish people for a sovereign national homeland but eventually expanded to include not only the borders of the historical Land of Israel but any land necessary to fulfil that ideal. At the very heart of the historical origins of the "Greater Israel" concept is the biblical vision of Eretz Yisrael, or the Land of Israel. This ideal extends well beyond the boundaries so fiercely contested and set following the War of 1948 and includes territories that have historically been associated with Jewish ownership. These include the West Bank, Gaza Strip, East Jerusalem, and the Golan Heights. This vision was developed by a number of well-known Zionists, like Theodor Herzl and Vladimir Jabotinsky, who championed the idea of the restoration of a Jewish national home in Palestine.

Their political work and writings created the idea of Greater Israel, which focusses on bringing back land that was historically Jewish and keeping it under the control of the state. Restoration and historical connection, along with religious significance, form the bedrock of Greater Israel ideology. Biblical texts and ancient geographic nomenclature pertaining to the land of Israel (in the proposed Greater Israel territory) are often employed to justify a claim over a wider land and, more specifically, to strengthen the historical attachment to particular regions, including those long neglected. In a broader historical context, Greater Israel is, thus, an idea, a geopolitical construction, and a more fundamentally embedded constituent of the geopolitics of the Middle East. Here, competing land claims, the religious importance of the territory, and historically constructed narratives give rise to conflicts and geopolitical disputes with geographic and territorial foundations. This historical context explains the enduring popularity and controversial legacy of Greater Israel. These have profoundly transformed regional geopolitics and interstate relations.

Strategic Motivations and Geopolitical Ambitions

The idea of Greater Israel has always been intertwined with the strategy and geopolitical ambitions that have shaped Israel's policies and those of the Israeli-controlled region. These motivations primarily focus on security, territorial expansion, and control over the surrounding population and land, which are central to Israel's strategy due to both historical circumstances and the current balance of power. It is still preferred for Israel to have controllable and defendable positions along all of its borders, albeit most of them have had no structural control or settlement for many decades. In addition to the numerous bulleted points focused on territorial expansion and confinement, this policy aims to ensure a significant Jewish population resides within the state, which are all clearly defined military objectives. It also represents a clear political and military goal: to achieve the security of the state and stability of the power.

Of course, Israel's geopolitical advances depend on gaining, consolidating, and controlling land and resources to have notable influence in the power struggles of Middle Eastern politics. Additionally, Israel's ambitions to control land and resources are influenced by its geopolitical history and contemporary power aspirations, which together shape a desire for control over a volatile region. The ideological objectives and socio-political control of the Greater Israel concept, along with ambitions to control land and resources, are intertwined with Israel's geopolitical strategy. In this case, the alignment of strategic goals and geopolitical ambitions clearly indicates that the objectives extend far beyond the mere acquisition of territory. Israel's influence in the territories and political theatre of the world is unbounded. It is important to underscore the multiple, sophisticated, and complex associations between security and territory that inform the geopolitical strategy and ambitions of Israel. All of these tell a single narrative that is the concept of a Greater Israel. Geopolitics clearly and seamlessly informs the strategy.

A historical ethnic people and the current nation state are primarily the shared foundational assets among the dominant internal actors within the United States.

Both the national and religious spheres inscribe this grand narrative, providing deep justifications for the internal political configurations of Israel.

There are also major complications concerning the expansion of territory to a particular region, and with that, the implications stretch beyond the immediate geography to the larger global geopolitics.

Territorial ambitions and Regional Implications

The ideological foundations and parameters The idea of an "Eretz Yisrael HaShlema" (Complete Land of Israel) represents a sophisticated ideology that is based on complex religious and historical conjectures, ultimately serving as the basis for a determinate quest for territorial expansion. This goal has far-reaching consequences for Israel's current borders and constitutes grave threats to regional stability, security, and chances of achieving lasting peace.

The attempt at territorial expansion will likely provoke and exacerbate world geopolitical tensions—adding to, not solving them—and add knots to the path for peace in many conflicts. This situation involves complex legal implications regarding territorial claims and delimitations, as well as incursions that violate international law.

It is more than just geographical; it has global political connotations that affect the policies of neighbouring states. There are numerous additional complex interconnecting factors that extend far beyond the scope of this summary.

Should Israel decide to annex part of what constitutes the heart of the Palestinian issue, it would fundamentally change both demography, the availability of natural resources, and power relations. These transformations would present significant challenges to the Palestinians and their neighbouring countries, upending the current geopolitical structure of the Middle East and requiring a reconfiguration of political alignments and power balances.

Furthermore, this territorial expansion would involve international players who are interested in the Israeli-Palestinian conflict and regional stability. It would also add a new layer of difficulty to the usual diplomatic dance and peace processes when it comes to conflict mediation.

Any annexation of new land would also make the enforcement of international law and United Nations resolutions even more difficult, as the balance of global power between Asia and America would be brought into regional affairs. The objectives of "Greater Israel" are typically divided into four general stakes, namely historical, regional geopolitical-territorial, global and ideological. In order to better understand the current and future geopolitics of the Middle East – a region experiencing multilayered regional contradictions and paradoxes – such complexities have to be unpacked. These desired objectives reveal complex and intertwined relationships, interests and power struggles in the region.

Domestic Politics and Ideological Drives

Political integration is the foundation of the ideological live veins that keep 'Greater Israel' alive. The political integration of religious, political, and national sentiments provides the foundations of the different streams of ideologies that comprise the various systems in Israel. The domestic political system is certainly a composite entity, rather than a political arena made up of a disparate collection of visions of the present, a plethora of ways to disseminate a national narrative, and a collective national hope for the future. This acceptance of the country's expansion to encompass a Greater Israel is self-evident. Within this integration, ideological sentiments can mobilise, shape public support, and influence social policies. The idea of Greater Israel, which includes religious beliefs about the land, the country's security needs, and strong national pride, is a major part of public opinion and unity.

Fortunately, the "Greater Israel" case, unlike most, transcends the usual political divides. Here, the extreme right and moderates alike echo, in their own different ways, a commitment to the primary objective. Additionally, the connection between local politics and beliefs is not just background noise; it actively affects political decisions about building and controlling settlements, annexations, and land management. The act of speech, in this case, mixes politely and impertinently, while coalition groups seek, in balancing several competing obligations and patriotism, to dominate the polydimensional space. Undoubtedly, "Greater Israel" also shapes educational curricula, the culture of community and political remembrance, and the people's national embodiment, collectively and almost seamlessly, as a community working within a time continuum.

Exploring domestic politics, ideology, religion, social attitudes, and parliamentary politics to explain the "Greater Israel" paradigm is a captivating enterprise. One may draw an almost instinctive understanding from the historical legacy and political landscape of Israel, the present oligarchical theatres, the enormous complexities surrounding regional aspirations, and the basic tensions of current politics. The realm of internal politics reflects a crucible where the hopes and fears of a nation coexist, out of which 'Greater Israel' emerges as a given reality.

Influence of International Law and Treaties

International relations and treaties shape the world politically, economically, and socially, and in the case of the Middle East, specifically, the notion of 'Greater' Israel. Within the framework of international and diplomatic relations law, the legal regulations governing the acquisition of territory and sovereignty have been contentious and controversial in the context of Israel's aspirations. Every international relations treaty and other passage of international law and treaties in the Middle East create ineffective regulations for the region. The residual colonial orders, the post-Great War mandates, and the subsequent resolutions of the world body have provided grounds for settling both the legal and illegal possessions of colonial Israel within the framework of international relations and treaty law. The rights granted by the UN, rather than the territory acquired through military aggression, have shaped Israel's occupation of Palestinian lands and other areas, as Israel currently controls all the land in the region. Geneva's Fourth Convention and the special humanitarian laws that protect people in occupied countries, especially in Jerusalem, have questioned Israel's legal responsibility towards the people affected by the settlements.

In addition, many bilateral and multilateral agreements, like the Oslo Accords and the Camp David Agreements, have attempted to resolve the disputes and build the groundwork for peaceful existence. However, the international political landscape and varying perspectives on the obligations of these agreements have rendered their application and enforcement challenging. With regard to value, the impact of international law and agreements goes beyond the soft politics of international advocacy and diplomacy. The way countries use laws or question important legal rules to push their political goals shows how law and global issues are connected. International legal and political relations, particularly the US, the EU, and many international organisations, focus on advocating for specific interpretations of international law, which adds to the complexity of the issue. The international law and international relations agreements do not simply focus on legal issues and international relations. They also focus on the morality and policy of the behaviour of nations, emphasising the peaceful coexistence, justice, and fundamental rights to which they aspire. Such information is crucial for understanding the inner workings of the Middle East.

Economic Interests and Resource Allocation

In addition to political and territorial ambitions, the idea of "Greater Israel" also has considerable economic aspects. This section addresses the economic factors driving the pursuit of this idea and the depth of resource allocation. Within the bounds of the 'Greater Israel' concept, economic factors play a primary role in the development of fundamental control over strategic long-term policies. The control and economic exploitation of resources—land, water, and energy—become primary objectives. This control also includes the development of infrastructure and the exploitation of trade routes, serving to strengthen the economy and consolidate power.

Within these objectives, the control of resources alters the domestic economic structure, which in turn affects the region's international relations. The pursuit of economic power and self-sufficiency, along with the control of the region's trade, supply lines, and infrastructure, becomes coordinated with the strategic vision of "Greater Israel". The various economic aspects must be analysed in a realistic economic framework to determine their impact on the various stakeholders.

By looking at how 'Greater Israel's' economy is organised and how its capital is invested and extended, the economy of 'Greater Israel' can be better understood. The relationship between economic capital, political power, and social advancement is essential to understanding the complexities of this paradigm. When assessing the social and geopolitical consequences of the phenomenon, it is important to consider the complexity of the economic and political relations involved. The economic relations and political power with socio-economic consequences, as well as the economic interdependence of the world, are the relations to be identified with the 'Greater Israel' project.

Impact on Palestinian Territories

The 'Greater Israel' project and its geopolitical aspirations significantly influence the socio-economic, political, and humanitarian conditions of the Palestinian territories. The socio-economic, political, and humanitarian crisis in the Palestinian territories, caused by the ongoing geopolitical confrontations between Israel and the Palestinians, continues to shape the region. The humanitarian crisis, the socio-economic and political situation, and the geopolitical ambitions of Israel and the Palestinian territories are influenced by the continuing Israeli settlements within the West Bank and East Jerusalem, influenced by the 'Greater Israel' ideology.

The ongoing crisis in Palestine and the people's access to land in Israel due to the wall's expansion have worsened violence and unrest in the territories. The building of Israeli walls cuts deeply into the West Bank and exacerbates the crises by restricting the access and movement of the people. The expansion of the wall exacerbates the crisis by imposing restrictions on the movement and access of people to the western region. The restrictions on movement and access to the economy for people in the southern region have resulted in individuals moving south to the region without access. Those who control the region, without consideration for the others, maintain control over land in other regions. Those who are in control of the southern part of the main region, both economically and socially, include those from the collapsed areas and other regions, as they maintain walls and structures that separate different parts of the population.

The outer region, located in the southern part of the area, witnesses the political and social collapse of its southern population. From the towers without walls, individuals impede movement, leading to a deep division in the south, while economically, people from the main region face collapse. The territories occupied by people without control suffer from the movement collapse, impacting social development and the socio-political stability of the outer main region. The absence of peace agreements has resulted in instability, which in turn encourages the need for further peace agreements – both Azeris and Armenians recognise this.

Hams Khalil and the Marshall Plan Development hold the belief that peace and development are inextricably linked. The development of the bankrupt Palestinian Authorities and Hamas focuses on each other, drowning out the other potential partner – Israel.

The aspirations of the so-called Greater Israel ideology have resulted in unbalanced development in the Palestinian territories, significantly affecting the potential socio-economic, political, and international relationships of the whole region. Each of these attributes of development must be analysed separately so that all other aspects of the Palestinian-Israeli conflict and potential developments are grounded in the realities of the region. The unbalanced socio-economic development of the territories and the rising new potential for social and economic development in Israel and the western world must be taken into account.

Arab-Israeli Relations and Diplomatic Maneuvres

The features described show that the socio-economic structure in the Arab-Israeli arises from a complex interplay between this region and other parts of the world. Six decades of the convolutions and cross purposes that these relationships have generated have achieved so much for the external world in terms of socio-economic change but precious little for the Arab-Israeli region. Its social and economic conditions have been influenced by geopolitical tensions that define its relationship with both regional and global players. Since the founding of the State of Israel in 1948, socio-economic life in the Arab-Israeli area has been molded by enemies that obstructed its progress and for which, geopolitical forces played a major role in shaping up its socio-economic development.

Peace efforts have shown the way An example Some examples of peace movements are: The Camp David Accords formed the basis for a look into achieving peace and coexistence between Israel and its Arab neighbors through political or diplomatic means rather than continuing to fight. Yet the issues of land, the return of refugees and security concerns continue to provide daunting obstacles to peace with Israel. The reaction of Arab states, alternating between hostility and accommodation has had a crucial impact on the peace process. The Arab states have historically had varying approaches to Israel, but these relationships were in part influenced by Israel's relations with the great powers, and other dynamics of the Cold War. Arab strategies, from their outright support in the Khartoum Resolutions to normalization agreements of recent years, have evolved as much as wider attitudes to the Israeli-Palestinian conflict.

Arab countries have either established diplomatic relations with Israel in a quest for peace or remained firm developed solidarity with Palestinians. The Palestinian problem is still the main issue in Arab-Israeli peace talks and between the Arab states themselves. Get breaking news and analyses on Major players and organizations influencing transatlantic news, covering efforts to counter extremism in Israel and the Arab world.

The ties between the Arab states and Israel endure, despite the continuing shifts or changes around one another. As the challenges become more complicated, players involved also have their own historical inheritances, power relations and ambitions which muscled regional order. But real change requires a more subtle and hybrid form of diplomacy and dialogue that accepts the land's real history and perceived history by all those whose conflicts shape it.

Military strategy and combat stance are essential to give an answer the description of the Middle East, just like in regards to the long lasting Israeli-Arab battle. Over the years of conflict, Israel's military has emerged as one of the most technologically advanced and strategically innovative in the world Despite a lack of strategic depth, early warning systems and more advanced warplanes have reduced its vulnerability to air attacks. The read moreCentral to Israeli military doctrine is the concept of deterrence, preventing aggression by convincing an adversary that there would be a high price for challenging Israel militarily. The complex task of defending against them requires Israel to possess a variety of military tools, so that in practice Israel maintains an extensive air force, operational missile defense systems, conventional ground forces and naval forces which is all required to be integrated into one single front for defense.

Furthermore, Israel's strategic military culture has been markedly shaped by its willingness to preempt and/or target operations, thus developing a self-imposed military doctrine favoring the prevention of threats. This principle is manifest in Israel's past wars, in which clear military action has been used to preempt serious threats. In addition, the Israeli military doctrine has evolved according to the asymmetrical reality regarding conflicts and the complexity of contemporary combat scenarios, which require a variety of responses. The Israeli defense system provides the ultimate example of complexity and adaptability, as it employs both conventional and unconventional methods — such as cyber warfare and counterinsurgency practices. The utilization of advanced technologies including unmanned (aerial) systems, precision-guided missiles and cyber to increase Israel's defensive capabilities underlines its capacity to preserve tactical dominance and battlefield awareness; epitomized as the inventive use of state-of-the art technology in Israel's defense structure.

Future Trajectories and Global Repercussions

The global geopolitics resulting from the future trajectories of the *Greater Israel* concept and its pursuit, along with its consequences, are as of now an unpredictable value. Given the continuing alteration of regional dynamics, the geopolitical consequences of a larger Israeli territory are highly anticipated to expand beyond Middle Eastern borders and impact the international relations system.

This vision has the potential to change the power dynamics within the region. Assimilating the 'Greater Israel' vision entails the border, sovereignty, and territory disputes within the region, which can lead to realignments in power with both risks and opportunities. This vision can potentially justify the removal and annexation of long-established borders in neighbouring countries, which results in new international dynamics to analyse. Empires such as the United States and the EU, among allied and neighbouring Arab countries, will be the new focus of international relations. Disputes will be of lesser value because of the assumed worth of the land. Regional conflicts will be the primary focus of international relations in the absence of civil wars. Israel being truer to its vision of a greater Israel will challenge new neighbouring countries and invoke the greater Middle East conflicts. Counteractions will invoke new alliances and civil conflicts within these new countries.

In addition, the interconnected nature of modern geopolitics means that changes of any sort within an isolated region are bound to create a ricochet of problems in the global scope of things, such as in the world's energy market or in transnational security. At the same time, the concept of a 'Greater Israel' has global geopolitical implications and is also deeply intertwined with the complex socioeconomics and humanitarian issues faced worldwide. These world socioeconomics and humanitarianism are gravely affected, particularly regarding forcibly displaced persons, by border and borderless community inter-crossed metamorphic economies. They relive established socio-economics and harmoniously discord the world socially. In addition, this geopolitically knitting structure may also become the basis of new borderless humanitarian provisions, new strategically structured humanitarian provisions, and new world socioeconomics and humanitarianism political development.

In short, the socio-economic development and global repercussions of the 'Greater Israel' initiative are major concerns for the world. To achieve a balanced geopolitical approach, the world's diplomacy must be modern, multidimensional, and orientated towards resolving moral conflicts.

6
Normalisation as Subjugation

Historical Context of Normalisation

A complex web of international links, vast geopolitical change, and the nature of diplomatic engagement intertwine with the background of normalisation. To underline existing developments, it is necessary to examine precedents rooted in history that produced the current climate of normalisation. Another important period was the years following World War II, when multilateral cooperation and peaceful coexistence between nations also became a model for the newly founded United Nations. It was a time of creation of many international agreements and organisations that were designed to promote discussion between the nations and also to limit tensions.

Following the Cold War, a clear east-versus-west division emerged, leading to the formation of relationships and alliances that continued to shape international relations. The 1970s and 1980s were a period that brought a form of détente, as nations attempted to improve the previously icy relations they had with each other. Meanwhile, territorial disputes and power rivalries led to a cyclical breakdown in diplomatic relations. When dropping the pen on treaties motivated by peace, such as the Camp David Accords in 1978, other gestures are associated with friendly relations between former enemies.

Additionally, the final breakdown of apartheid in South Africa during the 1990s led to an era of symbolic change and reparation that set a standard for countries attempting to mend their own deep-seated divides through diplomatic resolution. In the more immediate past, the tide of post-Cold War globalisation has utterly transformed international alliances and dependencies, forcing nations to rethink their diplomatic priorities and commitments. A review and reflection on these historical antecedents show that the theme of normalisation is intertwined with global events, power plays, and peace (or stability)-building.

Motivations Behind Diplomatic Engagements

Diplomacy is about more than protocol and etiquette; diplomacy involves a range of human urges. There are multiple layers of complexity associated with these motivations in the state normalisation process. One of the key drivers is the search for jobs and livelihoods. Countries usually have an interest in normalisation to enter new markets, reach critical resources and enable investments into their economy, increasing growth and welfare of the people living within them. This economic reasoning is often what triggers diplomatic interaction, as real money values can dramatically shore up a country's balance sheets.

The practical logic Regarding substantial economic incentives, I would conclude that even in very concrete amounts, but hopefully in estimates and projections, the relationship is still ruled by actual diplomatic conduct. Nations may join with one another for self-protection, creating alliances or partnerships that widen their geographic impact and serve as a defensive force. Strategic partnerships of this nature can have profound effects on diplomatic relations, as nations manoeuvre complex geopolitical terrain to maintain their independence. Second, strategic diplomacy can be based on cultural and social purposes as well. Countries could potentially normalise in order to cultivate cultural exchange and mutual understanding and therefore foster connections between people. It's a way of breaking down cultural silos and creating an environment of mutually supportive respect.

Furthermore, a need to resolve differences from the 'past' can drive diplomacy." Sustained efforts to 'normalise' relations provide countries with the opportunity to reconcile, forgive, and ultimately find ways to trust and collaborate. Finally, the search for common interest can motivate diplomatic efforts where nations seek to make alliances with those who they have political or ideological affinity with and therefore increase their influence on world affairs. Together, these factors highlight that diplomatic encounters are complex affairs involving a variety of economic, strategic, cultural, historical, and ideological issues. Understanding these factors is crucial in understanding the intricacies of international relations and realising that normalisation between countries is by nature a multi-factorial concern.

Patterns of Subjugation in Treaties

Diplomacy and treaties often operate like intricate mechanisms, seemingly promoting cooperation and shared interests but simultaneously incorporating structures of restraint. These tools of international relations govern state-to-state relations, but they may also perpetuate power imbalances and define the conduct of parties to a treaty. However, the skew in bargaining power among signatories is the fundamental mechanism that establishes dominance. "The relationship is invariably asymmetrical and unequal, and it is characterised by the retrospective and causal provision of benefits, rights, and resources from a more powerful empire or nation to a less powerful one, which erodes fairness."

A second major source of subordination rests on the vagueness and ambiguity that treaties typically are designed to build in. Vague language and open-ended clauses can lend themselves to significantly greater interpretation, favouring the big players in terms of enforcing unjustified uses of the agreements. This intentional vagueness privileges the more powerful part, giving him control over its practical application and direction.

Furthermore, there is often economic slavery veiled behind diplomacy. Bilateral agreements with financial dependencies or assistance can create conditions that cause the weaker partner to rely on the wealth and support of a more powerful trading partner. Such dependence creates an asymmetry of power and forces the weaker nation into submission to those of the stronger one in order not to lose essential economic aid, hence further limiting its capacity for independent decision-making.

There are cultural and ideological consequences of servitude as well. Agreements may reflect the senior power's norms, values, or worldviews in the junior state(s), with which it interacts in ways that do not necessarily chime with its identity. This coerced assimilation undermines the indigenous identity and self-determination of the subjected territory, promoting a sort of cultural imperialism without any open military aggression.

The hidden power architecture inherent in diplomatic agreements is fundamentally a complex dance of geopolitics, commerce, and culture. Appreciating these nuances and subjecting them to critical scrutiny are necessary for managing the intricacies of international relations without undermining other countries' sovereignty or autonomy at various levels.

Economic Connections and Strategic Exposure

In the model of normalisation as domination, economic interdependence and military dependency play a crucial role in structuring power hierarchies between states. With normalised pacts come economic ties that bind, creating opportunities for the strongest party to wield influence. This interdependence may be in the form of trade relations, capital flows, or energy dependence.

Weaknesses occur due to strategic disequilibria in the

structural dynamics of 'normalisation'. The stronger party can use economic interdependence as a means of installing a mechanism of domination, sometimes influencing the weaker one's strategic intentions. This pressure could be exploring realms in addition to economic ones, such as geopolitical blocks and coalitions or military partnerships. Thus, if the subjugated nation succumbs to the normalisation agreement, which is based on power disequilibrium, it will concede its sovereignty and independence.

Moreover, like all forms of economic dependency, resource extraction and uneven development could make the dependent nation further dependent on its dominant part. This generates a "dependency cycle," which makes it more difficult for a subjugated country to break the economic dependence imposed by normalisation agreements. This vulnerability will, in turn, make the weaker one vulnerable to being manipulated by their partner who is economically and strategically stronger, constricting even further its potential for autonomous growth and self-reliance.

The implications of economic entanglement and strategic vulnerability will need to be taken into account in any serious assessment of the long-term impacts of normalisation agreements. By acknowledging that there could be inequitable and negative consequences associated with interlocking economies and power imbalances, policymakers, scholars, and world leaders can more effectively navigate the complexities of normalisation as an instrument of dominance and control. In the end, attending to these economic and strategic levers within normalisation agreements is important for creating a world in which states exist as sovereign equals for mutual benefit.

Social and Cultural Dimensions of Conformity

A thorough investigation of the normalisation deal necessitates discussion of the cultural and social contexts involved. Cultural and social factors significantly influence the perceptions of nationals and the general public regarding trade negotiations. Normalisation typically involves accommodating and adjusting to different cultures, practices, and social contexts to enable entities to function together; however, it can also result in the erosion of local cultures, the subjugation of practices, and the loss of riparian self-determination.

Any project of normalisation that brings in foreign mentalities or ethical seeds may upset community structures and foment popular uprisings and resistance. Power relations between humanity can continue the processes of marginalisation in some groups. A critical look at these power relationships and cultural reconfigurations is necessary to understand the far-reaching consequences of normalising national as well as individual identities.

In addition, commercialising culture and heritage for political convenience leaves behind an ethical issue regarding normalisation. Cultivating a homogenised commercial culture to maintain diplomatic relations devalues and impoverishes genuine traditions. This state of affairs raises questions regarding who is empowered to speak for a people's cultural heritage and what ethical obligations are entailed in using cultural symbols in foreign policy.

We shouldn't underestimate the social implications of normalisation. Such agreements can also destabilise societies and increase divisions among them. The benefits of such agreements may flow to the elites and corporations, with marginal communities subject to exploitation and dispossession. This self-reinforcing cycle of inequality will exacerbate power divergences and even trigger social instability.

The social and cultural significance of conformity in the normalisation order must be grasped if we are to comprehend its essence and contributions to world order. Taking these dimensions apart is vital for promoting diplomacy, which allows for diversity and recognises the integrity of different cultural identities and social formations.

Case Studies: A Disparity of Partnerships

Whether the threat of game-changing decisions will lead to fragmentation – such as in past geopolitics or other animosities – remains a challenging issue. Some of those alliances illustrate the complicated geopolitics of collaboration in an environment of intense suspicion and competing priorities. Some individual examples and anecdotal accounts clarify the reality of these dynamics and the range of potential responses. The 1978 Camp David peace treaty between Israel and Egypt remains a seminal case in point. Though a breakthrough in Middle East diplomacy, the treaty also led to the departure of some Arab states from the Arab League in protest and made Egypt an outcast among many within it, including Libya and Sudan. Normalisation with Israel, even if it did contribute to stability, also acted as a source of bitter division for decades.

The 2017 Qatar crisis is again an example of how efforts at reconciliation can widen existing fractures. Several Arab states laid siege to Qatar, accusing it of supporting terrorism and getting too close to Iran – charges that had been made for more than a year. The disconnect in geopolitical alliances and efforts to normalise estrangement is symptomatic of this scenario.

The agreements reached between Israel and some Arab countries in 2020, which normalised relations with their former enemies, introduced an additional level of complication in the balance of power on the ground. Though these accords were greeted as an alternative route to peace and economic cooperation, they generated debate and controversy over how much they would actually help resolve the inequities and tensions that have long stricken the region. The differing reactions and the divided internal political situations in the Arab region shed light on the interaction of endogenous structures, exogenous interventions, and ensuing awkward alliances. The foregoing examples illustrate, however, how in seeking collaboration, the pursuit of normalisation could result paradoxically in increased fragmentation and alienation. With the complexities of the region and history of contentious relationships, a more complex evaluation of these potential relationships is necessary.

Reviewing the impact of such partnerships indicates that modern research would do well to take a more holistic view on normalisation work, understanding its complexity and the longstanding impacts it has.

Impact on Sovereign Autonomy

When evaluating the implications of normalisation, it is crucial to consider its effects on sovereign self-determination. The subtle implications of these normalisation agreements and protocols will have a knock-on effect on the sovereign autonomy of Middle Eastern states in a volatile geopolitical region. The consolidation of trade and diplomatic relations with major global economic powers in the region, among the states there, is now at a higher degree than maintaining equilibrium between economic autonomy versus diplomatic and foreign policy, which is fast disappearing. This secondary erosion in policy autonomy is even worse for states that wish to normalise relations with powerful global actors. The coalitions to ensure economic, military and political backing frequently require policy compromises which may limit the state's capacity to determine its policy issues unilaterally and hand over the state into an existential conflict between stakeholders of foreign policy.

There are also evident limits to unilateral policy choices in the normalisation framework. It is reasonable to claim that the unilateral policy choices of the middle powers will be strongly circumscribed by these overlaid relationships with leaders and other second-tier state actors during normalisation. Adherence to the convention of coalition support may narrow down choices for actors, especially if they seek socially salient, non-conforming options with which to ally in relation to a particular state at one moment in history.

A sovereign nation's right to remain uncompromised by external forces and agendas is fundamental. A state becomes more vulnerable to outside dictates as it submits to the conditions of normalising relations. This vulnerability can take myriad shapes, including being subject to particular trade regimes, governance systems, or military interventions that significantly hem in control over everything that goes on inside a territory and its border. What is more, undermining sovereign autonomy has implications far beyond regional squabbles and power politics. The fluid dynamics of normalised relationships can affect neighbouring states and set up new configurations of the balance of power. The aggregated declarations of independent sovereign states about normalisation shall be important in their own countries and for the collective will in the region; the outcome is bound to have commensurable impacts. Above all, rapid normalisation will have a severe impact on Middle Eastern states' sovereignty and the calculus of what they are willing to sacrifice in exchange for peace. How these countries negotiate these variables will not only determine their future but also the distribution of power in their region.

Critiques from Regional Thought Leaders

Criticism regarding the recent normalisation of relations between some countries and Israel from several Israeli advocates and regional opinion leaders is also receiving some accolades. For historical and geopolitical reasons, normalising relations with the country that has been the focus of the Middle East's geopolitical crises for so long is bound to receive criticism from all angles. Such criticism is highlighting these agreements as a detriment to the archetypal regional perspective on solving the Israeli-Palestinian conflict and, by extension, the Arab countries' control of the peace diplomacy efforts.

These same regional leaders, given recent interviews and comments, appear to be most concerned about the impact of normalising relations on the region's equilibrium and peace. Some appear to be most frustrated by the lack of real movement on fundamental issues, such as Palestinian self-determination and Jerusalem. It is also argued that such contacts can lend a measure of unwarranted parity to the most hard-line Israeli and Palestinian positions; therefore, to the extent that it can be rationally argued that the contacts would empower a more moderate position on either side, they would create a more intractable peace imbalance. Commentators often highlight the perceived imbalance in concessions made by each side in the normalisation agreements.

In some circles, particularly those receptive to the views of regional opinion-makers, it has been argued that the engagement rules might serve some strategic and economic interests, potentially hinging on Israel's position vis-à-vis other regional players. The agreement has been criticised on the grounds of unequal power distribution among the signatories and a lack of any goodwill or genuine desire for the collaboration to be long-term, as well as the effects on the region's security umbrella. Moreover, there are those who are concerned that normalisation, in the absence of any meaningful advances in the Israeli-Palestinian sphere, would effectively endorse the status quo—a status that many in the region consider untenable and inequitable.

Many critics of the region's normalisation have evidence of a lack of more substantive initiatives predicated on the potential for the erosion of a principled foreign policy, geographical solidarity with the cause, and trust and collaboration among the regional actors. In summary, the region's elites, with their considerable experience, are criticising the normalisation of relations with other countries and emphasising the complexity of the situation. From these criticisms, it has been proven that offering mutual understanding and partnership to the countries in the region is no simple endeavour, as it is highly complex and there are several different avenues to attempt to achieve this.

The effect of the normalisation agreements on the Palestinians

Consideration of the agreements normalising relations with Israel and some Arab states deepens well-known sore points and stimulates the Palestinian cause. There is rapidly growing disillusionment considering the abandonment of long-standing connections with Palestinian leadership and people. Additionally, people are feeling the lack of a resolution to the Israeli-Palestinian conflict and the absence of confidence in the role of regional players. The balance of the treaties impacts the geopolitical situation and Palestinian politics. The Peace Treaty has resulted in a deep rupture of the Palestinians, who, at present, have a homogenous opposition to the most appropriate strategy for the national cause. Of equal importance are the economic repercussions of normalising the territories. The threat of alienation will be acute for Palestine as the bordering states strengthen ties with Israel.

Hotly debated are the repercussions of the transition for development projects and the well-being of all Palestinians. The logic of normalisation, as well as short-term political and economic considerations relating to what is being sanitized—or rather, whose rights it legitimates— will remain an albatross for the Palestinians. This situation has cultural and social manifestations that trigger a surge of emotions and discussions among the Palestinian people. The struggle between identifying hope and betrayal and what resilience means to so many Palestinians has driven them to examine the core meaning behind "us", following the sympathy on the ground for a brighter future.

The answers to how the deals will affect the possibility of reigniting real talks between the Palestinians and Israel are all highly negative and yet to be seen on the diplomatic stage worldwide. The Palestinian division exemplifies Huntington's 'clash of civilisations' model. It has also further underlined the vital need to alter the course of diplomatic action and confront increasing international demand – to discharge legal responsibilities and uphold the rights and interests of the Palestinian people. In conclusion, the effects of the normalisation deals on Palestinian relations among themselves are deep and complex, extending to all spheres of Palestinian society and the international community.

So how to overcome these constraints—to respond to the short-term challenges while continuing the long-term effort to work toward a just and sustainable resolution to Palestinians' circumstances?

Theoretical Foundations of Asymmetrical Cooperation

The quest for the kind of asymmetrical cooperation that can accompany normalisation is complex, multi-layered, and shaped by deep disagreements over historical injustices, visions of power, and geopolitical realities. They are various and interrelated: Foreign policy The ways to build authentic forms of balanced trust between countries in a diplomatic partnership are many. The first step is to recognise and redress, in all their manifestations and dimensions, the historical injustices and power imbalances that might have played a role in breaking up the relationship between parties.

It is a commitment in all forms to truth and reconciliation that focuses on the past through dialogue, reparative understanding, and reconciliation. Additionally, equitable and beneficial structures and frameworks for economic interdependence serve as instruments of fair cooperation. Economically interdependent partnerships are designed to promote inclusive, balanced economic growth, lasting prosperity and development, and sustainable interdependence without forms of dependence that are exploitative and manipulative. Moreover, socio-political, cultural, educational, and inter-community exchanges significantly contribute to breaking psychological barriers and cultivating a culture of empathy, inclusiveness, and respect.

The development of such cross-cultural understanding is essential in dealing with stereotypes, prejudices and ethnocentrism, as well as in laying the groundwork for equitable and constructive collaboration. Furthermore, the active participation of civil society, people's movements, and non-governmental actors is of utmost importance to ensure that the cooperative efforts devised to protect targeted cross-border communities are inclusive of their voices and, more importantly, safeguard their rights. Such actors can also serve as advocates and promoters of trust, transparency and accountability in relation to diplomacy and normalisation.

This multidimensional cooperation—political, economic, and social—is the basis of just and durable relationships between the countries in the process of normalisation. Lastly, the principles of international law and human rights (i.e., the UN Charter), as well as the said cross-country cooperation, establish the framework of justice, equality and respect for sovereignty with which the cooperation is to be anchored on. Following the aforementioned principles is crucial for navigating normalisation pathways that foster genuine partnership and dignified coexistence.

7
Surveillance and Sovereignty: The Israeli Nexus

Surveillance Basics: A Worldwide Outlook

Surveillance as a practice has quite a history that spans centuries, covering various geographical regions and cultural traditions. Surveillance is fundamentally a trend used to describe the monitoring of people to look for evidence or knowledge, as well as interpretations of that evidence. It is now widespread in the Information Age, and its implications for global governance, privacy, and human rights have been profound. The spread of surveillance technologies, from closed-circuit television (CCTV) to advanced data analytics, has sparked controversies about how to strike the balance between security needs and personal freedoms. From the reliance of primitive cultures on direct observation to the use of cyber surveillance by modern nations, it has become an indispensable tool in the realms of geopolitics, intelligence gathering, and law enforcement.

In a world where governments and companies are using computers to monitor all of us, we need more technology that is designed in line with our values. The worldwide perspective on surveillance gives us a variety of motives, methods, and outcomes. Our investigation examines the antecedents and consequences of surveillance from memory across different societies, revealing a complex network of control, opposition, and sociopolitical configurations.

Historical Context: Israeli Intelligence Organisational Structure Development

Foundations The foundation of Israeli intelligence was based on the problems faced by early Zionism and state building. These Jewish militias, among them the Haganah, the Irgun, and the Lehi (Stern Gang), had been indispensable in gathering intelligence and clandestinely securing the borders of the community before the establishment of a state. The years of experience had laid the foundation for a far-reaching intelligence network that would become one of the pillars of Israel's security.

The need for an all-purpose intelligence service grew naturally when the state declared itself in 1948 because of Israel's immediate vulnerability to hostile neighbours and dangerous enemies. The 1950s marked a crucial period for Israeli intelligence, with the formation of Mossad, Shin Bet, and Aman. They contributed to the consolidation of Israel's intelligence establishment, whose tasks ranged from national security operations, both covert and counter-terrorism missions, to strategic analysis. Since then, Israeli intelligence has reconfigured almost constantly and been at the forefront of technology and strategic thinking for generations.

The 1960 kidnapping of Adolf Eichmann was one of its most well-known operations; it also performed hostage extractions, such as during a raid on Entebbe Airport in Uganda in 1976, and gathered intelligence from areas beyond enemy lines. Israeli intelligence performed well in the 1973 Yom Kippur War, as Israel managed to predict enemy moves on the basis of actionable intelligence. The integration of advanced surveillance technologies and cyber capabilities in recent decades has led to Israel becoming a significant intelligence power. Furthermore, the trinity of military, government and intelligence institutions – Israel's unique achievement of coordination – generates synergy that enables Israel's own doctrine of combined national security. The evolution of Israeli intelligence has been an agile one, morphing in response to evolving geopolitics and incarnating its enemies. A historical context for Israeli intelligence contributes to a deeper understanding of the relationship between security requirements and strategic processes and values.

The Arsenal of Technology: Sophisticated Surveillance Tools

The pace of technological change has also shifted the surveillance landscape, with all states – though to an uneven degree – having greater access to intelligence than ever before. In the shadowy world of Israeli intelligence—as in other parts of the country—precision-engineered electronic tools for spying are a demonstration not only that it is determined to remain ahead, but they also raise delicate questions about ethics and oversight. With the aid of up-to-the-minute satellite photography, low-flying drones, and high-tech aerial reconnaissance systems, Israel has created an impressive capability for surveillance that extends across borders and deep into enemy territory. In Israel, cutting-edge sensor technology and data mining are employed to enable intelligence agencies to run multi-dimensional real-time monitoring, helping sieve out vast amounts of information by collecting, filtering, and analysing the data.

This multiply-reflect (MR) SAGE approach provides decision-makers with actionable intelligence addressing the full range of security issues associated with military deployments, geopolitical trends, and possible threats. Furthermore, with advanced surveillance technology and analytic work, we can detect any possible security risk and take care of it before it becomes a threat. In addition to classic platforms, other cyberintelligence tools spread the lexicon of surveillance yet further—beyond the contours of physical terrain and onto digital networks and communications systems. Israeli cyberpower is essential to the conduct of more mature and increasingly sophisticated cyber campaigns for information, counteradversarial activity, and for enhancing our national cybersecurity. Its sophisticated surveillance techniques ranged from signal intercepts and cryptanalysis to offensive cyber operations, a further example of Israel's flexible approach to safeguarding its national security.

Arsenal possesses multinational technological capabilities in hardware and software that are exceptionally effective for operations. With training and research projects, personnel master the art of navigating through complex surveillance systems to glean useful intelligence. Israel is at the forefront of cutting-edge surveillance, which includes a combination of multidisciplinary expertise and strategic partnership with international market leaders to forge collaborative operations that cater for mutual security interests. The never-receding upgrade cycle of these surveillance systems bespeaks Israel's determination to try and keep up with new threats that come its way, the country forever longing for sovereignty in an increasingly complex world.

Cybersecurity and Espionage: The New Age of Conflict

In the contemporary reality of international security, it has come to pass that cyber war is a vital arena in world conflict. Cyber security and spycraft have never mattered more than they do today, with new technologies revolutionising the way countries spy and surveil. This new era of warfare transcends the physical realm. The battle on the virtual battlefield crosses over to the home front and back to your homeland. The widespread proliferation of cutting-edge cyber weapons and capabilities has led to a situation in which nations are not fighting only on physical battlegrounds, but they have also moved to cyberspace. Cybersecurity, once overlooked in previous national defence strategies, now shapes the architecture of 21st-century warfare. Protecting vital infrastructure, important information and government data from cyber threats is an inspiring reason to assert sovereignty.

Then, there is the undeniable truth that cyber espionage can yield priceless intelligence regarding its adversaries' intentions and capabilities, and exploitable vulnerabilities too. There are a wide range of strategic and tactical aspects to cyber espionage: political subversion, economic espionage, sabotage or attacks on critical infrastructure, services, etc. Cyber warfare does not simply involve states but a variety of non-state actors and disreputable rogue operators working to their own ends. This same ambience also has it that, therefore, over time, a lot of the criminals and current and would-be threats have simply taken to believing in a lack of accountability as an open cheque for their nefarious activities. They target the weak points of military cyber defences, disrupting their operations, disseminating false information, and undermining societal trust. Many people have prioritised election integrity, secure money movement, and private communication, highlighting the devastating effects of cyber threats on the solvency and sovereignty of nations.

The situation is made worse by the fact that, with technology evolving at unprecedented speed, AI, quantum computing, and the IoT are forming a rather complicated cybersecurity scene. Fifth-generation (5G) networks, the Internet of Things (IoT), autonomous systems, and so on—the future promises to bring both opportunity and challenge, as well as a broad spectrum of cyber vulnerabilities with associated threat vectors. The present scenario emphasises the need for resilient cyber defence and infrastructure, which similarly covers dynamic measures to defend against cyber-enabled espionage in other industries. In this evolving environment, international cooperation, diplomacy, and norms should play a role in promoting responsible cyberspace behaviour and constraining adversarial conduct. Establishing norms and promoting responsibility and transparency are critical to translating cyber capabilities into responsible behaviour consistent with ethics. Enhancing cyber resilience via cooperation, capacity, and response to protect against malicious cyber activities also contributed to strengthening the collective defence position. As advocates, technologists, and strategists collectively navigate the "circuitous combat domain" of cyberwarfare, they must adopt new methods and catalyse symbiotic relationships that foster defensive policies to ensure autonomy and sovereignty within this vastest of terra incognita in potential power struggles.

Sovereignty at Stake: How Surveillance Challenges National Autonomy

The rapidly evolving technology of surveillance has rendered the concept of national sovereignty unrecognisable. In conventional services, such as government surveillance capabilities, these technologies reinforce and shape the sovereignty of nations around the world. Private and public spy agencies end up monitoring private conversations, destroying a country's fundamental right to self-determined governance without intervention. The situation is even more dire in flashpoints, such as the geopolitically complex regions with long-standing cultural grudges, where surreptitious data collection further erodes already fragile political conditions. Moreover, with the growing nexus between the physical and cyberspace, the gap between legitimate security imperatives and unjustified incursions on national sovereignty will continue to narrow. Countries are attempting a delicate balance of trade-offs in what is essentially threading a needle between protecting citizens and the prerogatives of self-governance. But it's foolish to pretend that surveillance isn't an important tool for combating threats that are often the product of cross-border collaboration, such as terrorism and cyber warfare.

The interconnection of new security challenges necessitates a delicate balance between national sovereignty and collective security duties. But then there is also the uncertainty of allies or non-regulated actors using surveillance equipment – which only adds further to the sovereign dilemma. horizontal ellipsis In fact, interchanging data and knowledge sharing between countries gives rise to some fears concerning the preservation of national interests and confidentiality of sensitive information. Such alliances are meant not only to support joint security activities in some of the fields, but also these can end up directly or indirectly impinging upon a state's sovereignty and decision-making. There are ethical concerns regarding data collection and privacy.

Protections are raised, which can impact a country's independence. Governments of the world have been wrestling with a moral dilemma since 9/11 that tests the balance between people's right to privacy and freedom from unnecessary surveillance against security. It is an approach that balances security concerns against individual rights in a sensitive, graduated manner without compromising international law principles, such as transparency, accountability, and respect for established international regimes. The current debate around the impact of surveillance on a country's sovereignty makes it vividly clear that we must work to develop an equitable answer that respects the rights of nation-states as well as acknowledges our pressing security needs in today's world.

The Role of Allied Nations: Collaborations and Concerns

The word "collaboration" has many definitions when it

comes to Israel and its partner countries and surveillance capabilities: challenge, tension, and risk. Photo Without human rights protections from their home country, trained handlers receive no support from governments on the ground. Allies have historically played a critical role in enhancing Israel's surveillance capabilities through technology transfers, intelligence sharing, and joint operations. These partnerships, often shrouded in secrecy, raise questions about sovereignty, ethics and the broader geopolitical balance of power in the region. Collective security and counterterrorism are the narratives that design these common actions, but they also implicate human rights, privacy, and diplomacy. The delicate dance performed by Western intelligence services and Zionists requires critical examination along both legal and ethical lines. That does mean, however, (oddly) some very serious civil liberties issues – particularly around the sharing of surveillance data across borders.

Ultimately, patterns of relations among allies further transform regional fault lines and unwittingly constitute an environment conducive to instability and conflict in the region because they are coercive synergies. Mass surveillance tools used in a political or non-neighboring context demonstrate some vulnerabilities to these partnerships. Furthermore, the power imbalance could lead to overreliance on specific partners for intelligence or interpretation, compromising Israeli independent and strategic thinking. Changing alliances in international politics and the increasingly global availability of surveillance equipment make a comprehensive approach to cooperation important; one that doesn't only focus on current security needs but also takes sustainability and enduring cooperation into account. Now that national and international security concerns are intertwined, it is even more important to discuss them openly and inclusively. We must carefully strike a balance between pursuing shared security objectives and respecting the legal autonomy of all parties involved. This research underscores the role of discourse, regulatory frameworks and ethical guidance in how we come to think – both singularly and collectively -- about collaboration on matters such as surveillance and intelligence.

Instances: The Effects of Surveillance on Regional Stability

Surveillance has emerged as a crucial driver of regional order and a powerful tool for their geopolitics. The examination of representative scenarios provides valuable perspectives on how surveillance is impacting the delicate balance between power and security in different domains. A pertinent example is when it comes to the many forms of surveillance practiced throughout Middle Eastern conflicts, where state- and non-state entities increasingly use high-tech tools for spying and intelligence gathering. Such widespread surveillance in this area has ramped up suspicion and tensions among neighbours, putting a strain on diplomatic relations and fuelling conflicts. The use of espionage activities in the region poses a serious threat to territorial integrity and infringes upon sovereign rights, which can lead to controversy and diminish hopes for a peaceful resolution.

For an example of this, consider East Asia, where surveillance has escalated to the point that it is now essential for any concept of nautical security, largely due to territorial disputes. The application of unmanned aerial vehicles (UAVs) and sophisticated tracking practices has been driving maritime competitions, leading to greater confrontations and the weaponization of contested bodies of water. This strategy has riled up more than the region; it brings in other world powers and muddies diplomatic attempts. Secondly, the post-surveillance consequences on regional stability are unfolding in Africa, where the rapid deployment of surveillance technology collides with intricate socio-political contours. One very effective weapon of the state to suppress dissent and coerce is surveillance, fomenting low-grade conflict within countries through perpetual disorders, and thereby the easier commission of abuses of human rights. The continued provision of surveillance infrastructure by external actors can exacerbate long-term repression and prolong conflict, even as it complicates life for democratic forces. These cases illustrate the complexity of surveillance and regional stability, and it highlights that addressing the broad-minded impact of mass surveillance is critical.

Ethical and Human Rights Considerations

The ethics of surveillance and intel work are key, particularly when there's a human rights angle to them. Such rapid technological advancements blur the morality of surveillance. And the collecting and monitoring of billions of pieces of personal information raise significant concerns about privacy, consent and freedom. The extent to which surveillance not only threatens national security but also the civil liberties of both citizens within and outside our territories must be explored.

The debate at this micro-level of ethics, Droit-Volet says, usually centres on the principle of proportionality: that any encroachment on privacy or impingement on individual freedoms has to be justified by an acceptable and proportionate aim. Especially in the area of surveillance, it is often unclear where privacy rights end and national security interests begin. More broadly, surveillance could be used secondarily to smother dissent, discriminate, or mould public discourse in ways that would be unethical under current international human rights frameworks— making clear the importance of having strong ethical frameworks.

The human rights implications of permanent surveillance are immense. Intrusive monitoring violates a number of freedoms, such as the right to privacy enshrined in human rights conventions and freedom of opinion, expression and assembly. There is a growing global consensus that the need to find an equilibrium between security imperatives and human rights is essential for maintaining democratic ethos and social peace. But upholding this balance depends on clear legal regimes, oversight mechanisms and procedures for accountability to make sure that surveillance is ethical and in line with human rights.

There's also a normative dimension to the transnational implications of spy games. Given the current global interconnected nature of society and crossing-border data, extraterritorial reach for surveillance not only raises complex ethical issues but also brings about difficult legal questions. I'm just thinking about issues of state sovereignty and people beyond the borders of these countries. The international community faces the challenge of maintaining a delicate balance between state security interests and global human rights protections.

In general, the conversations on ethics and human rights outside of those surrounding surveillance will have to be holistic in nature – inclusive of other perspectives that take into account fundamental freedoms and allow for convergence globally on justice and inclusivity.

International Law and Regulation Regimes

The fusion of public international law with regulatory regimes is especially important in the nexus of surveillance and sovereignty. Within this framework, the challenges posed by technological advancements and machines making decisions that impact autonomy necessitate a thorough examination of the existing legal framework. This heart of darkness on the one hand and substance of light shed at better angels on the other animates not only legality but also how such surveillance technologies will be deployed and may be employed under international law — including how states can maintain an edgy balance between security imperatives and human rights exigencies.

And the United Nations has been a key space for crafting and imagining international legal norms on surveillance and sovereignty. There are a variety of bodies and entities right across the UN system—including the International Court of Justice and the Human Rights Council—that work to develop laws on these issues. Treaties and agreements set down basic principles upon which states conduct themselves in relation to surveillance laws and national sovereignty, for instance the International Covenant of Civil and

Political Rights, as well as the Geneva Conventions.

Furthermore, surveillance practices in specific regions influence the regulative context. It is provided by institutions such as the European Union's Agency for Fundamental Rights (FRA) and the African Union Commission, which advise states on what sort of surveillance laws should be in place in their regions, considering various regional subtleties and sensitivities regarding sovereignty vis-à-vis human rights. Access The interaction between global and regional legal instruments illustrated should serve as a reminder of the dynamic nature of surveillance discourse and the need for full compliance with multi-layered rule sets.

Moreover, the intertwining relations of extradition relations, MLATs, and diplomatic considerations further muddle the complex one amongst surveillance, sovereignty, and public international law. These pacts establish the rules of intelligence sharing and cross-border operations, showing how important legal cooperation can be in minimising international blowback from surveillance activities. Sanctions for violations of international law are necessary to create a disincentive against ever-too-broad surveillance practices that encroach on the sovereignty of other nations.

We need to further explore and sort out the roles of international legal systems in a world of rapidly evolving technological landscapes. The challenges have developed over time, and this means that policymakers also need to reconsider the fit of current treatments in order to strike a balance between national security considerations, sovereignty and individual rights when facing matters such as data protection, cyber warfare or the use of AI in surveillance services. This changing landscape illustrates the importance of continued transnational exchange and collaboration vis-à-vis surveillance and sovereignty's intricate legal panoply.

Final Thoughts: Weighing security and sovereignty

Security and sovereignty are vital aspects of contemporary geopolitics. Security versus sovereignty In the terrain of contemporary world politics, security and sovereignty are perennially thorny issues. Traditional concepts of national sovereignty have become obsolete due to the rapid advancement of surveillance technology and intelligence capabilities. As countries start to tighten security due to a handful of recent threats, this is frequently the result. The need for a system that effectively reconciles such important factors is paramount for balancing global peace and state-based entities.

At the heart of this is the realisation that security and sovereignty are not disparate but dialectical. Of course, protecting national borders and the people in them is important, but so is the principle that a sovereign state has the right to determine its own future. Such a need to manage these imperatives simultaneously calls for a complex mix of legal, ethical and diplomatic dimensions.

Under closer scrutiny of this fragile balance, however, we will see that international law operates as a framework, outlining the limits within which states can decide what their security dictates. The charter of the UN and many other human rights charters are also responsible for the international regulation of the behaviour of states, such that no security measures can despoil or violate enough nationally recognised sovereign rights of states. Therefore, making an effort to respect these tenets of law would help avoid encroachments on state sovereignty by invasive surveillance programmes.

At the same time, we need to structure a systematic approach to ethical questions about surveillance and security. We need to carefully consider the metaethical questions that result from the dismantling of privacy, civil rights, and democratic institutions. It is essential to slip the line between security and individual freedom gently in order not to disturb the legitimacy of the state or trust-building. This combination of moral and practical considerations that emerges during the framing process highlights how challenging and precarious it is to achieve a degree of equilibrium.

Moreover, the discipline of international relations is ripe for discussions of the security/sovereignty nexus. Dialogue, cooperation and transparency among states are remedies against potential friction between different security aims. Collaborative efforts to enhance the standardisation of surveillance measures, intelligence sharing, and mutual understanding can foster alignment around security goals that also respect sovereignty.

In the end, there is a need to incorporate security imperatives into sovereign rights by building a more general culture of accountability and principles. Part of this model includes robust oversight mechanisms, assessing the impact of surveillance and active engagement with civil society and international entities. Authorities' receptiveness to legitimate concerns could increase confidence and legitimacy of security measures in the PR discourse on sovereignty.

The question is how the struggle for security can be reconciled with due esteem for national sovereignty. Neutralising threats of all kinds should be compatible with maintaining the independence and sovereignty of nations. Therefore, it is the responsibility of the international community to incorporate these imperatives into organisations and practices, transforming them into a clear framework that views security and sovereignty as complementary aspects that underpin global order.

8
The Diplomatic Facade: A Look Behind Closed Doors

Historical Context: The Evolution of Diplomatic Engagement

International relations and geopolitics are two realms of study that benefit from the influence of diplomacy. This influence has been integral throughout the range of documented international relations. In the history of diplomacy, the first recorded instances are found in the primary societies, in the form of envoys sent to secure, negotiate, or resolve treaties and alliances. The foremost pivots of the dynamics of the world were the evolutions and adaptations of diplomatic practices and protocols, the influence of the balance of power, and the new challenges and opportunities in the international realm.

One of the earliest forms of diplomacy was personal—an envoy, often trusted, would negotiate or find means to keep channels open in an alliance or potential conflict. The growing complexity of society made the need for embassies and codified diplomatic practices a necessity, and thus a modern form of diplomacy was born. This fact was recognised by the growing presence of international and multilateral institutions. Westphalia, in 1648, became the first landmark in diplomacy, as it recognised the modern system of international relations based on state sovereignty, and thus, began the promotion of diplomatic practices, treaties, and multilateral diplomacy.

This foundational principle still supports today's diplomatic practices. The 19th and 20th centuries also included varying degrees of modification in diplomacy as a result of industrialisation, colonialism, and ideological conflicts. The institutionalisation of diplomacy as a profession was reflected in the exponential growth of diplomatic missions, the increasing number of members of a diplomatic corps, and the growing professionalism of diplomatic services. The introduction of new communication tools, starting with the telegraph, brought to diplomacy unprecedented speed and efficiency in communicative decision-making and crisis resolution.

The new forms of diplomacy, negotiation, mediation, and peacebuilding responded to the increased complexity in diplomatic relations that characterised the period after the Second World War and the Cold War. The relationships also included non-state actors, transnational problems, and global interdependence. The increasing complexity of global interdependence and the challenges within diplomatic relationships contributed to the overall complexity of these issues. Consequently, the historical evolution of diplomacy has a bearing on the foundations, practices, and constraints of present-day diplomacy.

Key Players and Influencers: Identifying Stakeholders

In the complex web of diplomatic negotiations, the first step to understanding the dynamics of the web is to identify key players and influencers.

State and non-state actors have a large stake in the conduct of international relations and diplomacy. Politicians and policymakers are the most prominent and take charge in formulating the primary policies on bilateral relations. There are also influential advisors and intermediaries who, although not in the limelight, exercise considerable power and influence on policy due to their advice and control of negotiations. More than ever, it is also necessary to appreciate the contributions of large non-state actors in trade and diplomacy; their concerns about trade, market, and investment make them very active and powerful participants in diplomacy.

There are also societal and cultural stakeholders such as scholars, journalists, and members of civil society who are influential in the indirect regulation of diplomacy, who at the same time adjust the public interests and debates on diplomacy. With respect to the focus of this book, understanding the stakeholders in the region's diplomacy and international relations would provide a balanced understanding of their interests and power configurations. These stakeholders include political leaders from the surrounding countries and global actors who possess power and a deliberate influence over the region. Understanding these stakeholders is pivotal in comprehending diplomacy and the political choices these leaders make.

Analysing the historical relations, partnerships, and conflicts of these specific stakeholders can further clarify their positions and perspectives, as well as inform their roles—whether positive or negative—during potential diplomatic breakthroughs. When there are stakeholders to consider, there is also the need for a detailed consideration of their respective elements and of the range and extent of their resources, abilities, and means to shape and bring about particular results.

Appreciating and understanding the dynamics of relative

power, collusive and cooperative frameworks, and strategic partnerships helps us understand the complex systems of diplomatic relations. Furthermore, the internal characteristics of the stakeholders, such as the administrative and bureaucratic arrangements, the interest groups, and the focused and specialised influence groups, are critical to understanding the issues and problems that determine and explain the involvement of these actors in the sphere of diplomacy.

Thus, identifying the key actors, along with their relationships and positions in diplomatic relations, will clarify the various dimensions of these relations and the issues involved in negotiations. Understanding the various relationships and interests of all actors in diplomacy will enhance comprehension of the situations, relations, and mechanisms available for diplomatic efforts. This understanding will assist in resolving the problems and issues present in complex multilateral and bilateral relations, as well as provide insights that will aid in determining the strategies needed to achieve the desired outcomes in diplomacy.

Bilateral Agendas: Deciphering Intentions

One of the primary aspects of international affairs is comprehending the purposes behind many policies and programs; this certainly applies to bilateral policies. The strategic, economic and geopolitical parts are all components of the basic substance of bilateral policies, most or all of which are affected by an amalgamation of history and presence. Only an intimate knowledge of past and present can lead to a nuanced understanding of all sides' motives. Studying the past interactions of these two sides is one of the most important ways to gain insight into bilateral relations. These historical relationships and contacts may provide clues for understanding the current motivations and objectives of the parties involved.

Analysing the development of relations through treaties and disputes may help better understand the long-term objectives and expectations of international system actors, as well as their treaty partners. Moreover, the "core idea" of national interests and strategic goals is used to interpret the original intention of bilateral relations. Governments articulate in a calculated way their respective national interests and declared aims in foreign policy. Although those public policies are commendable for promoting straightforward external relations, a careful analysis would likely reveal that they imply the opposite of their stated intent. Examining only public and purposely undisclosed intentions provides a partial picture of intentionality.

Even more difficult is disentangling these effects from compact two-way influences. Regional alliances, global power plays and cross-border friendships add to the tangled web of motives behind diplomacy. To fully understand the magnitude of this analytical frame, we have to find out who these multilaterally operative actors are. These global hegemonies, cross-regional alliances, and regional partners also operate multilaterally along political-strategic lines between "partner states," with economic factors being equally decisive. There is no such thing as "purely diplomatic" without economic considerations, since exchanges, investments, profit flows, or simply money relations are powerful political weapons in our time. For bilateral agendas, focused consideration is necessary for the economic components—trade ties, monetary investments, and economic interdependence. Both dossiers require a comprehensive decision that, among other things, connects a historico-geopolitical overview, common knowledge, official thinking, and elements of significant importance. To truly understand diplomacy, we must distinguish genuine national interests from convoluted hidden motives and manage conflicting influences.

Negotiation Dynamics: Strategies and Tactics

There is a complicated orchestration of strategies and tactics, which underpins the pace and dynamics of diplomatic engagement.

The international relations diplomacy process serves as the mechanism through which nations navigate the complexity of international relations and pursue mutually beneficial interests amid competing interests and world views. Ultimately, negotiation is the art and science of strategy and tactics, based on the intelligence of diplomats, the political objectives of the countries concerned, and the type of conflict. Three of the keys to knowing and understanding the dynamics and basics of negotiation in diplomacy are power, leverage, and mutual gain. Military, economy, and geography are the powers of strategy in diplomacy. The diplomat needs to be extremely cautious in the dispensation, use and exercise of the power of negotiation, and it also requires a proper skill for understanding the power balance with other diplomats. One can interpose negotiation tactics to gain a competitive advantage. The techniques used in negotiations include taking the initiative, setting the terms of trade (framing), manipulating public information, and being selective about what to say. The consultants who do these tasks should be very knowledgeable and sensitive to the cultures, histories, and psyches of the countries involved while still achieving their major negotiating objectives.

In addition, a close inspection of various kinds of negotiations—including resolving disputes and striking trade deals involving several countries—reveals that effective negotiations require extensive preparation, the right sequence of discussions, and emotional insight. Additionally, small actions that foster an atmosphere of cooperation and comfort are crucial for initiating successful negotiations, as progress cannot be made if people only respond to emails. Diplomacy is the game of making logical and reasonable, pragmatic positions or decisions ... But at the end it's all about emotions. The most effective negotiators are those who understand human nature in its various forms, including the influence of feelings and diverse perspectives, enabling them to carefully consider their actions before making a decision in the realm of diplomacy. As negotiators, their ability to listen and understand is what produces successful negotiations that foster relationship building. This focus on diplomacy's most basic tools and their execution, however, reveals that the essence of negotiation is rooted in both history and politics, as well as being an inherent aspect of human nature. There is, in every diplomatic process, a subtle performance in which negotiators juggle three forceful instruments – language and time, as well as the softer instrument of concession – to map out a pleasant picture for both their countries.

Public Versus Private Posturing: Understanding Discrepancies

The difference between public and private utterances is particularly important and requires attention in diplomacy. It is vital to understanding the challenges of international diplomacy in public and private negotiations. At its core, the contradiction reflects the complexities arising from the cross-interests of political and diplomatic actors. Speaking to different types of people is one major reason for that variation. Public statements are generally fashioned in a way that is intended to resonate with a domestic and international audience— to express opinions and secure backing for given policies or positions. Public diplomacy is generally described as idealistic and expressive of moral legitimacy and national solidarity. While behind closed doors negotiations are pragmatic and based in the realpolitik of negotiations, interests dictate concessions made on the political battlefield.

The difference between public and private positions also underscores the tightrope walk that diplomats and leaders must perform. Diplomatic relations also tend to involve a bit of performing and speaking on a tightrope, blending public remarks with the ultimate aims of the country unless those aims come into direct conflict with core diplomatic needs. Secondly, this difference highlights the international alliances and rivalries in global politics by simplifying speech and action into routines, mechanics, and formalities that help maintain a balance of power for both sides while also facilitating various outcomes beneficial to any single country.

In addition, the distinction between public and private language serves to impart a sense of the psychology of diplomacy. It must be evident that it is the perceptions and impressions attached to a narrative that are the ones that help craft the diplomacy of a country. Hence the distinction between public and private speech elucidates power dynamics, influence mechanisms, and perceptions. Patterns of power and perception control provide valid reasons to suspect motives, assess the legitimacy of a diplomatic promise, and estimate the likelihood of a country changing its position on key issues. This power to see patterns and anticipate the global path of a country in diplomatic issues is most useful for policymakers, diplomats and analysts who seek order in a complex domain known as international politics.

Knowing the real difference between public and private posturing pops that backfield wide open, granting access to the complexities of diplomacy that is always close to becoming wholly cynical about how nations come to deals. Once the differential postures have been recognised and analysed, decision-makers can get a handle on why actors are doing what they do, creating an opening for more nuanced thinking and better choices in support of public order and even the world.

The Impact of Media on the Construction of Diplomatic Narratives

In the field of world diplomacy, media has a significant responsibility because of the ability to shape and determine the direction of the public and the diplomacy of the targets involved. Media is able to capture, influence, and control the actions, policies, and people in international diplomacy. Thus, the influence of media in this area is profound and complex. Media is, first of all, a channel of information. Media reports covering diplomacy, its negotiation, and geostrategic developments keep the public and the world informed. Media analysis and commentaries on diplomacy detail the positions, tactics, and philosophies of the spokesmen, negotiators, and diplomats involved in the processes. The media informed the public and exercised control over the actions of diplomats and policymakers. In addition to this, media framing of diplomacy and public policy issues in the form of opinion constructs a perception of international policy. The choice of words, style of writing, and focus of a text can present an image of international diplomacy that is controversial. An issue can motivate the public to either support or oppose it.

Thus, governments and diplomats attempt to control and manage their media and public perception. Furthermore, the media can cover diplomatic activities with either greater understanding and transparency or with greater misunderstanding and ignorance. The media's coverage and reporting are essential in helping the public form reasonable and accurate opinions about international relations. The media can report in such a manner as to create and escalate conflicts and barriers to diplomatic relations. Beyond influencing public opinion, media coverage can influence the attitudes and opinions of governments and diplomats. The media constitute a powerful tool of advocacy and influence in international relations. Constructive relations among countries depend on the media's portrayal of their leaders and on the media's coverage of diplomatic relations between countries. The media can either undermine or enhance the cooperation and understanding relations of states and, therefore, the diplomacy of states. The media's influence on diplomacy and the portrayal of the relationships between governments is significant and considerable. The impact of the media on international relationships is every public and political actor's challenge, and their responsibility is to ensure responsible and adequate media regulation.

A comprehension of the role of the media as an instrument of diplomacy is critical for the understanding of its role in the discourse of the entire world and the practice of global diplomacy.

The Role of Diplomacy in Unofficial Communication Channels

In the practice of global diplomacy, the role of the diplomatically unofficial is considerable, and yet, it remains hidden. Unlike the public diplomatic channels, the unofficial diplomatic dialogues enable a diplomat or a government official to engage in private and public communications with other actors in the public sphere. These bypass public scrutiny and best facilitate the consideration of alternative means of diplomacy and conflict resolution and bridge the understanding gaps with and between social and political enemies. These informal and unofficial contacts devoid of diplomatic intrigue and levers of politics would be anathema to the political diplomat. Such contacts would prompt the consideration of suggested political and diplomatic "bottom lines." The absence of diplomatic intrigue and political levers enables a diplomat to deliver political "bottom lines" devoid of the traditional political or diplomatic restraints of the public. Such would allow a diplomat to bypass polite consideration of bureaucratic or diplomatic structures. In the absence of a formal structure, the diplomat is able to articulate a political "bottom line" without diplomatic intrigue or political restraints.

Historically, backchannel diplomacy has assisted in crossing extreme geopolitical deadlocks via the Cuban Missile Crisis and the Iran-Contra scandal, where breakthrough secret negotiations were achieved contrary to the most optimistic predictions. Today, the presence of backchannel communications, characterised by unorganised informal discussions and secret dealings, is ubiquitous in the context of major diplomatic impasses and protracted wars. Such informal communications uniquely generate and facilitate soft and friendly discussions unencumbered by diplomatic protocol. The dialogic nature of backchannel processes allows diplomacy to go beyond the primary focus of interests and directly approach the needs, fears, and hopes that are often suppressed in traditional diplomacy. The potential scope of backchannel diplomacy is greatly positive for conflict settlement. However, the secretive nature of backchannel communications can lead to serious issues, including miscommunication and the lack of responsibility to ensure that the information asymmetry does not work to the disadvantage of the less powerful. The absence of these informal discussions can continue to impede efforts to address the essential structures of mistrust and suspicion.

There are ethical issues related to the intersection of backchannel communications and diplomacy due to the geopolitical balance of power. For example, there are concerns around the possible consequences of backchannel diplomacy and the circumvention of democracy, the democratic deficit, and democratic accountability. Achieving balance between the possible advantages to diplomacy of cloaked negotiations and the accountability to democracy is the central dilemma of backchannel communications. However, the deep paradoxes of the present world order have led to the importance of developing new forms of diplomacy designed to promote active participation in democracy, combat illiberal forms of democracy, promote peace, and foster international stability.

The Role of Economic Incentives in Addressing Aspects of Diplomatic Engagement

The practice of economic diplomacy is also one of the most evolved today. Economic incentives are a regular part of international relations. Leveraging economic incentives is an effective means of promoting national interests and encouraging international cooperation. Economic incentives such as regulatory or trade treaties and foreign aid are an important part of the measurement and design of interest at a national level. The Fact is Used to Create a Relationship While the use of economic incentives has long been used for building relationships and maintaining and augmenting diplomatic relations, for resolving disputes, and as a tool of influence in world politics. Economic incentives are used to establish and strengthen relationships.

Countries can create favourable attitudes, economic partnerships, and relationships by providing not only economic aid but also trading opportunities. They would not only help the drive for economic growth and development but also strengthen relationships and ensure diplomatic peace. In addition to this, such economic projects can also help bring about peace and end conflicts. In conflict areas, economic assistance and investments can support the rebuilding of these countries after the devastation of wars, as well as address humanitarian crises and lay a basis for sustainable peace. And availability of diplomacy. Policy Diplomats: Countries that are performing economic game changes along with diplomacy can be seen...as a common feature in major economic growth nations. Economic initiatives can also play a crucial role in pursuing specific strategic objectives and initiating desired domestic policy reforms. This can be achieved through trade pacts and investment deals in which states rewrite the country's rules while exchanging significant resources, thereby advancing their geopolitical interests. We can move forward on shared priorities and tackle difficult geopolitical issues, all with the help of economic collaboration and trade partners. There will be conflict. Material incentives can create power imbalances and vulnerabilities.

However, the instruments of economic statecraft should not be predatory, as doing so would violate the norms of ethically equitable diplomacy and lead to worse relations and additional ethical dilemmas. Someone who comes to appreciate the subtleties of diplomacy will realise that it's not just a trade in transactions. They are intricate instruments that shape the tides of international relations and, in doing so, define active commerce in the diplomacy of economies amidst other actors in world affairs. They influence how economies trade to develop relations, help critical transactions in the world economy, and take part in global commerce.

The Study of Diplomatic Success and Failure

Diplomacy possesses a certain elegance, characterised by the balance and nuances of intertwining negotiations, agreements, and periods without compromises. The study of diplomacy, along with the nuances of achieving success and experiencing failure in complex relationships, is considered an art. This section addresses the positive examples of other diplomatic efforts and provides an analysis of failures, clearly defining the factors that contribute to success or lead to failure. Diplomatic success is the result of a convergence of will and interest. Success in such events can be defined as the willingness of the parties to work together, and success lies in the presence of new innovative approaches to the dialogue, which, in the end, yield creative problem-solving that becomes the central component. In these predicaments, balance is achieved by rational and enlightened altruism that openly defies the pressure of self-interest to give an answer to the problem.

In the first place, diplomatic failures illustrate the consequences of neglecting the factors of collaboration, as well as the level of communication, calculation, and trust required to work together. As with the lessons of failure, so too are the lessons of power and the ideology and history of the respective diplomatic engagements. In balancing the successes and failures of diplomacy, the most relevant case studies to consider are those of peace accords, trade agreements, and security agreements. In these cases, we can observe the clearest balance of the numerous factors involved in the contextual dynamics, as well as the most significant geopolitical influences. If we must say something good about external actors in mediated diplomacy, we can mention relationships. Each of these diplomacies should give us something positive to say in reflecting upon the relationships that have been maintained. In opposition to the relationships we have described, we can say with confidence that all of the peace, trade, and security diplomacies need to avoid rough assessments.

When constructing reasoning for responsive strategies for future engagements, it is also essential to understand the destabilising consequences of lost opportunities in diplomacy. The study of diplomacy's successes and failures is a tool best used to understand the nuances of present-day international relations. Through the analysis of historical context and current events, diplomats and policymakers can take a positive approach to determining globally equitable, sustainable, and inclusive diplomacy strategies.

Future Prospects: Assessing Potential Outcomes

One of the most urgent duties of international diplomacy is to look ahead and map out what comes next. Global diplomacy is a complex and fluid system, which can be shaped by various – and often conflicting – forces, such as historical grievances or the alignment of political or economic objectives. Looking to the future, understanding geopolitics involves considering where the world's attention is shifting and the potential trajectories of its major actors. In the immediate term, what makes sense is to engage on this probability of ending festering and violent vendettas and proxy wars.

Historical records and recent policy changes examine the feasibility of reaching meaningful agreements and implementing peace processes. We also need to consider the emerging powers and non-state entities that will influence future geopolitics. The growing power of these new actors has challenged established forms of power and global shifts. Second, how possible outcomes are weighed will always be a function of the nature of regional and global alliances.

The shared interests between the core countries and the KIs will require a clear analysis about how, if at all, geopolitical alliances can change, which influences other alliance dynamics. And emphasising these historical alliances and their reasons will provide some basis for speculation about likely new alliances and common actions that may characterise future diplomacy. Economic motivations and trade dynamics are also important predictors in policing diplomacy. Countries come together and collaborate mostly because of the material interests. Though as yet only a source of conjecture and theory, examining the economic links and the trade dimensions indicates perhaps what is influencing those trade prospects in a diplomatic arena.

Moreover, the promise of digital diplomacy and a series of recent technological advancements is to redefine conventional modes of diplomacy, communication and alliance-building. Every time we factor in potential variables and benefits, a cross-sector lens that brings historical, geopolitical, economic, and innovative perspectives into conversation becomes more apparent. The intricate nature of the system of world diplomacy requires a strong understanding of its internal workings to anticipate likely eventualities. An intense and analytical study of the emerging dynamics of the world diplomacy system, along with questions about future expectations in world diplomacy, is essential.

9
The Role of the International Community

The Importance of International Diplomacy

The importance of this sphere in terms of preserving the world geopolitical balance is unprecedented. The most fundamental part of international relations is communication, relationships, negotiation, and strategy among global organisations and countries. Intergovernmental cooperation aims at common goals and resolves conflicts for the sake of world peace and security. The economy, history, culture, differences and power of the countries determine and shape international diplomacy.

The variety of the configurations of international diplomacy can be used to develop channels through which one or more parties may communicate, mediate and find common ground on numerous issues. These range from trade, security and human rights to various components of the environment and diplomacy. International relations include traditional state-to-state interactions, as well as the relationships existing among new forms of non-sovereign de facto states, multinational corporations and the institutions of global governance. These network ties are further amplified by the latest international diplomacy forms – like non-governmental organisations. The latest and the best-constructed diplomatic structures supplement international diplomacy. The past actions cast a crucial legacy on the current political map. The historical background of intervention in international affairs is important for comprehending the development of international diplomacy.

World politics Writing, diplomacy, and international relations in general have been shaped by significant events, including major wars and revolutions, political betrayals, mass shifts of power, and the course of history itself.. 6. Detailed Animated History. We must therefore examine history to understand the transitions that, positive or negative as they may be, have formed contemporary international relations today. Textbooks and histories of international relations provide the landmark events in diplomatic history, as well as insight into shared – if never settled – problems or lessons that must be learnt anew every time they are not heeded. Therefore, any effort to comprehend the complex and varied elements of contemporary diplomacy should inevitably begin with a look to its past.

The Historical Backdrop: One Dead Example and Some Other Legacies

In order to comprehend the geopolitical landscape of today, we need to know about global interventions and influences in world history. The Middle East has been the scene of major conflicts in international relations throughout history and the subject of great power influence and intervention. The Middle East's historical global conflicts and strategic value have engendered great-power competition — from colonial times to the Cold War.

Key among these was the Sykes-Picot Agreement of 1916, which created, for the first time ever, an organisation that reshaped Middle East map lines. The Sykes-Picot Agreement spawned our modern nation-states, but it also made possible the eruption of nation-states that are still uncontrollable today. The post-WWII era saw the duel of the superpowers, i.e., the USA vs. the USSR, which chose the Middle East as an arena of competing eminence. During the Cold War there was backing for proxy regimes, and militarism and funding these only deepened the inter-regional rivalries and provided an added layer of ideological separations within the regionality of the sequential countries themselves. Yet another pivotal event in this series of events is the 1953 CIA-sponsored "overthrow" of Prime Minister of Iran Mohammad Mossadegh (the first minister who was democratically elected) and restoration to power of the Pahlavi dynasty. This interference would pave the way for most Middle Eastern nations to be visited by such foreign intervention. The end of the Cold War and Gulf Wars, especially the 2003 Iraqi coup, established a new geopolitical order and has added to new sectarian rivalries, old or new, inside and around these Middle Eastern countries.

The changes had led to enormous social and political transitions, turning the architecture of power on its head and widening the already existing fissures. But besides military shifts, economic and diplomatic changes have shaped the region's course. The environment of the target countries has been shaped by their economic dependence on sanctions, trade relationships, and aid. Understanding the rich diversity of past interventions and influences is a prerequisite to confronting the present challenge of the international community to the Middle East. It is also important to know the history of intervention and influence in the area that colours both diplomacy and conflict resolution, causing them to be even more difficult to achieve.

The United Nations: Resolutions and Realities

The United Nations (UN) is the leading international organisation responsible for the maintenance of international peace and security, the development of friendly relations among nations, and the promotion of social progress, including better living standards and universal human rights. The UN, in the context of global conflict and crisis, is central in issuing resolutions to mitigate the geopolitical challenges of the world. The UN General Assembly, comprising the different member states of the UN, is the arena for free and thorough debate on a range of world problems.

Moreover, there exist five permanent members of the Council with veto powers, meaning the Council holds a decision-making top-tier role for all issues of peace and security. While this part of the UN's mandate indicates its importance, realisation of the UN's mandate does not come easily. Its ability to effect peace in the world, and especially for its warring members, is conditioned on a number of issues, including, for one, the self-determination of the members in contention and the dominance of foreign political relations between member states. In some circumstances, the UN's restrictions on political cohesion to effectuate its decided mandate have encountered the UN's culminating power to maintain order. In addition, the limited effectiveness of the UN's back resolutions is always a direct consequence of the order in the Security Council. The power of the Council's permanent members in veto positions especially influences the order of the Council in the political cases of "cherry-picking" resolutions to undermine the UN's role as an adjudicator in international affairs, and in the disputes of Ukraine and the Middle East can also result in a loss of an impartial "neutral" position. Finally, the hostile engagement of the warring parties brings more significant challenges to the designed UN measures to exhaust the mandate of measures.

There is a lack of agreement among member nations, and this can lead to weak and ineffective resolutions, causing frustration in transforming the situation. However, the United Nations resolutions are effective in addressing and managing world problems and solving them with diplomacy. But to do so is very complicated and you must take into account the complex politics of the world and the cooperation of many individuals. This relationship is the United Nations' strength and weakness in international diplomacy, as the balance of idealistic goals with the practical application of laws is the reality of conflict in the world.

Key Players: The Role of Superpowers

The focus of superpowers in geopolitics has always been a major issue. They influence and affect more than their own nations, shaping the behaviours of entire regions and the outcomes of great global struggles. Regarding the Middle East, the powers of the United States, Russia, and China will be more relevant at all times than the European Union. They all wield immense political, economic, and military influence with undeniable consequences. For instance, the USA has been and is still one of the main players in Middle Eastern politics, including its military as well as diplomatic involvement.

The alliances and rivalries among these states have played an important role in the stability and security images of the region. Middle Eastern powers, such as Iran and the United States, vie for influence and compete against other states and regional players like China. Russia's strategic priorities and selective backing for Middle Eastern governments, as well as its (Moscow's) implication in regional wars, can affect the region differently.

The increasing economic interests of China in the Middle East and the attendant rapid spread of infrastructures (including construction works) to which China is providing financial support can transform, making room in geopolitics for a new player. The rise (if still limited) of the European Union (EU) as a diplomatic and economic matter remains in the mix. What these powers can do in the world (US, Russia, China, and EU) is to either stabilise or destabilise the region. The increasing presence of these superpowers also completely restructures security and economic and political interdependency among states in the regions as well as globally. The Middle East experiences a set of interconnected subsystems and other regional actors as well. It is clear that understanding these superpowers (especially the US) within the context of Middle East geopolitics is important, as most subsystems and situations in the region cannot be significantly separated from them.

Coalitions and Alliances: Shifting Dynamics

On a world scale, intersecting geopolitical interests and historical- and strategy-based concerns create new alliances at the formation or rearrange coalitions. In the evolving world, the creation and dismantlement of coalitions and alliances are displayed in the delicate symmetry of power structures and conflicting interests. Alliances are the proof of partnerships in international relations, whether they are military and security alliances or trade blocs." The dynamic of these relationships reflects the shifts in power between them. Changing geopolitical tides, rising power centres and shifting security threats are all catalysts for complex relationships. The old Cold War alliances have shifted as new, rising powers disillusioned by the status quo vie to create geopolitical relationships of their own. The rise of economic interdependence among world states is a primary cause for changes in alliances and coalitions. Trade Globalisation and economic interdependence are key to international affairs; they drive cooperation and competition among countries. Global economic ties can be an avenue for cooperation, but they can also lead to alliances among nations trying to exercise political power.

Moreover, forming alliances is quite a matter of shared ideas and values. Common values like democracy and human rights, as well as all other kinds of governance, can help bring together countries moving in the same direction. Yet different values and interests can undermine alliances and make it easier to break down as well as reorder the world. The flexibility of alliances can present both advantages and disadvantages for decision-makers. The complex structure of alliances requires extensive historical knowledge, a deep understanding of the region, and a clear future game plan. It is of great significance to regulate and forecast an alliance's behaviour, especially when safeguarding fragile equilibrium as well as its corresponding stability. The formation of alliances/coalitions will repeatedly determine the order of the global system. How alliance formation and shifts matter is where the nature and effects of alliance movements inform modern foreign policy for effective global governance structures.

Challenges of Consensus Building

It is profoundly difficult to build consensus in international diplomacy, and that tends to be an obstacle to rapid action. One of the reasons is that joining countries or entities have diverse interests and priorities. Each has its own history, political drivers, and strategic interests at stake, making it very difficult to come up with common measures. Furthermore, changing network power can affect the extent of influence in international institutions, which could drive contentious bargaining and inefficient outcomes. Striking an agreement in such a complex matrix of interests requires maintaining balance and engaging all parties.

However, there is another giant barrier that has to be overcome in arriving at a consensus – cultural coupling to phenomena between the various ideologies, cultures and countries. These differences have also shaped where the candidates stand on major issues, like human rights, the economy, and security. That's going to mean a lot of talking and understanding between the two sides, along with an understanding of why each party appears to be doing what it's doing. Furthermore, there are old fights and past enmities among the states that could hinder cooperative approaches to consensus. International bodies often lag behind in responding to global crises due to their slow action.

Long-winded talking shops and bureaucratic hurdles that stall the making of coherent responses to a crisis reduce the effectiveness of international interventions. Furthermore, the situation is further complicated for consensus-building by the intersection of economic interests and geopolitical strategies in countries attempting to protect their own interests or stakes in international political negotiations. The internal challenge of building a consensus is also being confounded by the emergence of non-state actors and transnational networks that are powerfully shaping world politics. Their involvement is problematic because non-state actors may have interests or objectives that differ from those of traditional diplomats. "Fake news" and propaganda in a digital media landscape are other big obstacles to having an informed and commonly grounded freedom of expression."

The world can function a lot as it slogs through these murky issues of war with its own people, but middle-power states should step up to bolster confidence, transparency and diplomacy. Being inclusive and recognising the legitimacy of other perspectives can encourage a more coherent consensus-building process. It takes patience, perseverance, a real willingness to work with others for the greater good and that skill of arriving at consensus where you actually get something done."

Humanitarian Concerns versus Political Agendas

World affairs, entangled in layers of complex geopolitics, often struggle between the demands of charity and those of geopolitical convenience. Although it is grounded in the avoidance of human suffering, in the protection and promotion of human rights and minimum standards of humane behaviour, humanitarianism stands for something very specific. "But it turns out that compared to the firmly grounded political interests and strategic wagers for nation-states in a specific circumstance, these advantageous purposes can turn into a chain [sic] of self-contradictory logics and targets."

There is essentially a paradox: while there is moral pressure to alleviate human suffering, there are also political interests at the national or regional level, and often, decisions are driven by pragmatic concerns about how to save lives. This clash of worlds is often, on the international stage, subject to fierce argument and policy choices.

Furthermore, power relationships, ideological conventions and historical constructions all too frequently mask the meeting of humanitarian needs with political pragmatism. While humanitarianism is ostensibly neutral, informed only by an imperative obligation to save lives and provide aid, it may be compromised and exploited by politico-military actors pursuing strategic goals. This event also represents a reckoning on how the generosity of humanitarians can stand up to the ugliness and contradictions of realpolitik, where self-interests and power politics reign. Even the conflict between humanitarianism and political opportunism could be seen on a global scale in some of those crises—wars, natural disasters, waves of refugees.

The calculus in these cases between alleviating human suffering in the short term and maintaining grand geopolitical postures for the national interest is near impossible to make. However, the interests of humanitarianism and its norms typically lose out to national security, financial gain, and geopolitical influence. Thus, it is only through dialogue and cooperation and principled actions from all members of the international community that such a contradiction between humanitarian imperatives and political considerations could be managed. It would force us to reconsider not just so-called best practices for humanitarian intervention but also our ability to locate a space between the two clashing demands of our moral responsibilities toward those who suffer and the realities of power politics. Only if they have an acute understanding of such inescapable, interconnected ties can international actors hope to nudge incrementally toward more effective and principled humanitarian action, as that must necessarily be conditioned by the crowded theatre of politics.

Economic Leverage and Sanctions

Economic instruments and sanctions are frequently used by the international community to try to influence state behaviour, particularly in situations where it is felt that they have strayed beyond acceptable international standards or the need for peace and security. The central tenet of this strategy is that inflicting significant economic hardship on a target country can lead to changes in its behaviour, policies, or even the removal of its leadership. Sanctions may take different forms, from a trade embargo or asset freeze to economic sanctions, which also include technology transfer restrictions, etc.

These counter-terrorism measures can cause quite extensive negative impacts on the population and economy of the targeted country. It is imperative to consider the expected humanitarian consequences when policymakers deliberate use of economic leverage and sanctions. And second, even if the goal is to counter offensive behaviour, there needs to be more thought about collateral damage when it is regular people who get caught in the crossfire of these actions. How effective those measures will be will also have to be closely scrutinised, since experience has shown that sanctions do not always have the intended effect. In some cases, these efforts aim to strengthen internal solidarity and resistance, resulting in prolonged confrontations instead of compliance. But economic pressure and sanctions have a way of also leading to overwhelmingly complicated geopolitical headaches.

Regional and international powers could seize on the chaos to advance their agenda, stoking current tensions and widening divides. Moreover, the execution of sanctions relies heavily on cooperation from an array of actors—neighboring countries, trading partners, and financial institutions. A nonobservance of the sanctions regime, so it can be said, will undoubtedly serve to substantially diminish its deterrent effect. Iran stands to illustrate the larger complexities—and controversies— of using economic clout to punish and isolate a country. The imposition of harsh sanctions on Iran's oil and financial sectors elicited divergent reactions from different foreign states, as the gaps between their strategic priorities were made clear. Supporters argued that the sanctions were necessary to prevent Iran from developing nuclear weapons, while opponents claimed they had caused undue suffering to the Iranian population and that they failed to accomplish their goal. Lastly, effectively using economic pressure and sanctions as a weapon against a target is always nuanced, based upon the humanitarian fronts and factors of geopolitics & economics that come into play. We must heed the lesson of unintended consequences, as the stakes are too high. How much economic pressure to exert while protecting innocent people is a constant struggle for the international community.

Case Studies: Successes and Failures

There have been great examples of international community intervention that we can reflect on regarding their success. But the enormous success of peacekeeping in the Balkans in the 1990s—a peaceful international response led by the UN that arrested calamity and transitioned to a post-war stability—was also fraught with challenges. The cooperative effort of this intervention demonstrates that, with a clear purpose and the commitment of pooled resources, multilateral action can be effective. At the opposite end of these justifications is the truth that international actors who failed to act to prevent genocide in Rwanda cast a long shadow by refusing to make a decision. The 1994 disaster illustrated the human cost when world powers fail to respond at greater speed or with more effectiveness. We should be ashamed, but let this tragedy teach us what happens when we ignore complex geopolitics and humanitarian crises.

The recent forays into Middle East calamity only underscore the awkward issues of foreign intervention. Regime change has been discredited after Iraq and Libya, with quagmires over post-conflict stabilisation and the difficulty of helping societies rebuild themselves. It is a hopeful sign that the solution to effective intervention is not only to address crises of immediate security but also to construct institutions and government. The Kosovo intervention, dictating double standards like it did and having problems like all wars do, was a successful humanitarian intervention in that it stopped more deadly levels of violence and eased the suffering of repressed people. It also illustrates the delicate balance between respecting sovereignty and alleviating human suffering, a reminder that we, as nations, possess the power to effect change. In rare detail, this case report provides some insight into the complex and problematic nexus of international intervention in conflict/crisis with the humanitarian system. In each instance, the dilemma is one of competing priorities and forces—"competing agendas," as it were—in an environment of state control and management, with humanitarian imperatives potentially at odds with political constraints. Let's analyse these mistakes and challenges; let's relearn the basic facts about condition-led international engagement—how indispensable a diplomatic vision is, how crucial strategic coordination is, and how irremovable support for global peace and human dignity justifies one another.

The Prospect of International Involvement

The shifting international landscape and its effect on prospects for international engagement are important. The fast-moving and increasingly interconnected global stage has far-ranging implications for the topographies of multiple geopolitical problems and conflicts, not least in the Middle East. As we enter into an era of intricate political relations, it is becoming more necessary than ever to start visualising the kind of models that could be implemented to construct various paths of communication and diplomatic gestures with other countries.

Strategists and policymakers will need to closely study the fuller dynamics of power relations and economic interdependence, as well as the new risks they entail. What has happened in the past and is happening now, as well as new opportunities, shapes the future of international intervention. The way we will utilise these technological advancements, which are influencing us and our communication, is through conflict resolution. So as new tools bring digital diplomacy into a new century and artificial intelligence takes on a bigger role in policy decision-making, it would be about time for one to further learn these ethical and strategic approaches to engagement. Furthermore, the advent of cyber warfare and its place in relations among nations calls for a fresh look at survival systems.

These temporary alliances and blocs help redraw the world in another direction. And as traditional zones of influence collapse, we see new nontraditional allies, or blocs, begin to form, which are in line with a more multipolar world order as well. This change shows bonding and dialogue can overcome common problems with shared goals. Additionally, non-state actors and civil society organisations already play a significant role in shaping global agendas, contributing to a reordering of diplomatic relations that appears more favourable to empire-like structures. The influence of NGOs, social movements and activist networks in the policy process is real enough to prompt rethinking international regime participation. In an age where the unarguable effects of climate change are becoming impossible to ignore, all focus has turned across the globe to environmental diplomacy. Therefore, the world is engaging with contemporary sustainable development programmes and pursuing collaborative efforts that aim to resolve environmental crises in the coming years.

Diplomatic discussions will focus on the potential for managing climate-related conflicts to promote energy cooperation and encourage the development of green technology. The ultimate path upholds human rights and humanitarian laws. In our discussions in the world, we are too often compromised by realpolitik, but a shift of focus to human values rather than traditional foreign policy can help us arrive at a more just and fair global order. The convergence of these factors underscores the urgency of formulating a principled, comprehensive agenda for IC engagement in the long term.

10
Building a Cohesive Arab Strategy

Introduction to the Challenges

Formulating a cohesive strategy towards a host of Arab countries is fraught with nuance to consider. Geopolitics, internal conflicts, varying levels of economic development, and social and cultural backgrounds are all significant factors to take into account. Collectively, these serve to shape decision-making and frustrate consensus around regional vectors or interests. However, tension between states, borders, and fluctuating ideological inclinations leads to cohesion problems and also clouds the prospects for unified Arab action, as inter-Arab tension hinders the development and implementation of a combined strategy. Such obstacles, if they persist, cause division and stagnation in our march forward together. Dealing with these obstacles is crucial to forming a united strategy that meets the expectations and needs of all Arab nations. Grasping the scale of these challenges can allow leaders and decision-makers to counter division strategically and promote togetherness.

Historical Background for the Arab Reawakening

The Arabs have been looking for unity since the fall of the Ottoman Empire. The notion of an Arab front has been an ideal as well as a struggle historically, often animated by external pressures and racked with internal divisions. The creation of the predecessors and ancestors of today's Arab states followed directly from this. The early civilisations of the Mesopotamians, ancient Egyptians, and Nabataeans were also major influences on the Arab world; many of these values spread through Saudi Arabia. The sense of community and belonging together was derived from this resemblance. The various conquests by outside forces, such as the Ottomans and later European colonialists, disrupted the emerging unity, leading to the disintegration of the region into colonies and protectorates, each with different and sometimes contrasting fates.

The shape and traces of the regions became deeper lines, scars, and contours during the creation of nation-states after World War I, when borders were drawn without considering historical relationships or communal homogeneity. Despite these historical roadblocks, the concept of pan-Arabism gained ground in the early 20th century, with promises (at least in theory) to unite Arab nations under a common destiny on the strength of charismatic leaders like Gamal Abdel Nasser and Michel Aflaq. Responses to personal or political motivations among the countries are obstructing the progress of building Arab unity towards actualisation, especially considering that since 1945, when the Arab League was established to achieve unity, it has been mired in conflicts. The Arab League has remained mired in conflicts since its establishment. They understand the burden of history and colonial heritage on today's Arab order. "Those currents remain in the murky past, but today they continue to shape perceptions, aspirations, and predicaments—with much to consider as we try to make sense of coherent endeavours that would enhance collective interests and regional stability."

Analysing the Contemporary Geopolitical Landscape

The modern-day Arab geopolitical environment represents a plethora of intricate and fluid variables. Among such factors are power struggles between regional and interventionist foreign policies and the presence of non-state actors. The region faces classic conflicts that drive it through Israeli-Palestinian relations, as well as new ones, as the ramifications of foreign power interests come into play. And, naturally, one cannot rule out the malign impact of militancy/terrorism that has evolved security models and ruptured interstate relations. Furthermore, the Arab world is divided along ideological, confessional, and political lines, which hinders the establishment of a strong state and instead promotes divisive principles.

The Arab Spring has not simplified regional dynamics, however, and a resurgence of nationalistic sentiment muddles the situation even further as it encourages cooperation among some states but also competition with others. Moreover, incongruities in wealth and resource distribution persist to dictate regional relations, forging alliances while also sowing discord. Apart from the reshaping of global markets due to changes in the energy and commodity landscape, the Arab world is now experiencing broader geopolitical shifts, underscoring the importance of maintaining a united front. In a whirlwind, the changing nature of public debate and activism through memes and clicktivism has led governments to face increased scrutiny from their citizens at home and from other nations abroad, which in turn influences their decision-making. Finally, new international trends, namely climate change and dynamic alliances, all add to the complexity of the Arab geopolitical space, which calls for adaptive strategies and vision. Awareness of these complications is critical in shaping an Arab strategy capable of successfully managing the complex field of present-day geopolitical uncertainties.

The Impact of Political Fragmentation

One of the most challenging problems facing the Arab world is political fragmentation, which has long prevented the region from acting as one entity to achieve common strategic goals or navigate through a complex geopolitical theatre. The nature of the electoral entities in the Arab world is broken down into a chaotic number of parts, leading to disunity and conflict between interests, leaving them unable to play an effective regional role. In addition, this amount of fragmentation has served to both dilute the standing and clout of the Arab states within international organisations as well as create avenues for external actors to take advantage of such divisions to advance their own strategic interests. The Arab world has failed to produce a united political front, making it susceptible to outside interference and influence and severing its capacity to make its own future.

Lack of political unity and commonality has also delayed the possibility of successfully addressing common challenges, such as economic growth, security threats and societal advancement. Arab nations' divergent foreign policies and confrontational alliances have helped instigate instability and opened space for outside players. Moreover, the lack of a single cohesive political voice has limited the region's ability to project its common vision and interests on the world stage, and the result was an opportunity missed for cooperation with other global powers. Political fragmentation also reflects internal governance by seeding discord and stifling promising social, economic and cultural projects that would otherwise be able to advance the Arab world. It is necessary to consider the impact of political disintegration when planning and implementing a unified Arab strategy to address challenges on multiple fronts. The Arab world can pursue a common response that seizes opportunities, overcomes vulnerabilities, and unleashes dynamic regional transformation by recognising and addressing fragmentation.

Formulating Strategic Objectives

Strategic goals are the key components to a coordinated Arab strategy. Amidst the current geopolitics, Arab countries are confronted with a multitude of challenges that encompass political instability, economic divides, and security issues. With clear strategic goals, the Arab world can work towards unity and advancement. While doing so, it's important to focus on well-defined goals. Such objectives could include promoting regional stability, sustainable development or cooperative security. In addition, strategic goals should aim to promote a conducive atmosphere for intraregional collaboration and cooperation in key areas, including trade, technology, and innovation. Cooperation can enable the pursuit of such ambitious yet crucial goals. It is therefore necessary to build broad frameworks that enable Arab nations to work together. This can include setting up a common task force, high-level summits, and defence agreements.

Through harmonising their strategic goals, the Arab states can jointly marshal resources, skills and capacity to confront these obstacles more effectively. Moreover, the establishment of a common vision among Arab nations and clear strategic objectives to achieve it may serve as an antidote for external hegemonic aspirations in line with enhancing the region's role and position on the world map. Additionally, it is crucial to align these strategic priorities with the broader principles of justice, human rights, and sustainable development. What's more, using cultural and historical relations can be an asset to define strategic targets that express the dreams and the ideals of the Arab people. It may help develop a collective identity and destiny that supersedes any one nation and paves the way for a more prosperous future together. In the end, forging strategic goals from the diverse aspirations and organic needs of Arab states must take account of external pressures and opportunities against rigorous calculations. The Arab world can carve a path to resilience, prosperity and influence in an increasingly globalised landscape by establishing clear and realistic targets.

Leveraging Economic Cooperation

The use of economic cooperation as a mechanism to bring about unity and progress is an important cornerstone for unity in the Arab world. The synchronisation of economies in the Arab world holds significant potential for harnessing shared interests and promoting sustainable development. By building bridges across diverse societal challenges, which the region faces, economic integration would be a driver for increasing inclusive growth and resilience. It is crucial for economic cooperation to move beyond the limitations of mere bilateral trade agreements and adopt a more comprehensive approach to mutual, cooperative growth that aims to be as optimistic as possible while also remaining grounded in principles of equitable distribution.

At the heart of this work is identifying pivotal industries that can be mutually reinforcing and synergistic. Joint ventures have numerous opportunities to foster mutual benefits in energy cooperation by constructing infrastructure, sharing technology, and transferring knowledge. Arab states could benefit from each other by harmonising their national economic policies and strategies towards a common regional vision, leveraging their collective comparative advantages to overcome individual vulnerabilities.

Furthermore, interest in intra-regional investments and a favourable investment environment are also the basis of economic interconnectivity. You can do so by adopting common regulatory frameworks, simplifying cross-border trade procedures and developing standards and compliance processes that ease barriers to intra-Arab trade and investment, and thus improve market access and liquidity. Also, efforts to promote both small and medium-sized businesses and entrepreneurship will lead to job creation and economic empowerment across the region, which will encourage innovation and diversification. In addition to tangible benefits, economic cooperation also involves establishing financial mechanisms and institutions to support collective development projects. Whether through infrastructure financing or R&D investment, such mechanisms can unlock resources to drive catalytic projects that tackle shared problems and exploit new openings. Furthermore, adopting sustainable development and recognising the importance of environmental stewardship in economic activity elevates the long-term sustainability of cooperative actions. In a nutshell, the capitalisation of economic cooperation within the Arab World will require something more than just trade: a mindset that moves to relinquish old grudges for comprehensive development. It requires a move away from personal interests towards a collective approach focused upon the advancement of all, inclusion and resilience. By pooling resources, knowledge and hopes together, the Arab countries can pave a path to opening an avenue of connectedness and prosperity for an entire region guided by economic soundness and shared and expanded capabilities.

Harnessing Diplomatic Leverage

Diplomacy is the most important source of realising national and collective interests, so that through it countries can negotiate these relations skilfully, by which basic international relations are conducted. At a time when creating an integrated Arab strategy is essential, diplomatic leverage matters above all else. Once again, we explore the different facets of diplomatic engagement, but now with an appreciation for the imperatives that drive its effective use.

Using diplomatic leverage effectively is crucial, as it involves judiciously promoting collective Arab interests to the world, ensuring our sovereignty and autonomy, and avoiding self-defeating actions. This aspect calls for an integrated approach towards bilateral and multilateral diplomacy. Arab states can convey a united aspiration for regional stability, economic development, and political progress by negotiating shrewdly and presenting a firm stance on the international stage. Part of diplomacy is building relationships with foreign nations and regional blocs that lead to a favourable environment for trade and cooperation. Through such alliances, Arab states can extend their sphere of influence and establish common projects.

Diplomatic initiatives serve as channels for addressing common problems and conflicts while facilitating dialogue and building consensus on vital matters. Secondly, effective diplomatic leverage involves establishing a nuanced understanding of international relationships, requiring the ability to navigate the significant complexities of the world stage. This implies developing a diplomatic calculus suited to the changing nature of international politics, such as engagement with rising powers, managing rivalries among them, and coping with external pressures. Furthermore, their active involvement in international organisations and bodies provides Arab states with a venue to promote jointly defended interests and fashion regional and national narratives and global policies reflecting the cause of choice. Moreover, diplomacy is not limited to what we traditionally think of as state-to-state affairs but rather involves a wide variety of actors, including non-state entities, civil society, and diaspora communities.

Capitalising on such platforms allows the Arab world to build networks, develop and increase its soft power, and drive cultural diplomacy, building links and common understanding. Through these non-traditional means, the Arab states can convey the mosaic of their cultural heritage, many past achievements and modern accomplishments to heighten their international position and impact attitudes. In addition, such exchanges lead to deeper people-to-people ties which, in turn, help create lasting partnerships and relationships. In sum, utilising diplomatic capital is essential to the task of forging a unified Arab strategy and paving the way towards a cohesive and effective role on the international stage. Arab countries have the ability to transform this potential into a robust region that follows global norms and upholds its principles, thereby enhancing the strength of Arab nations.

Cultural and Social Cohesion

Cultural and social unity in the Arab world is of great importance for the adoption of a common strategy. The weave of customs and culture, history and values is crucial to cementing a collective sense of identity across the Arab world. The following discusses the extent to which cultural and social solidarity influences the development and execution of an integrated Arab strategy. This shared set of traditions, languages and historical events is a collective thread that links numerous Arab communities together; it trumps borders and sects. Applying this institutional unity can not only reinforce identity and pride; it can also develop a shared awareness that supports cooperative conduct. Preserving and promoting the cultural heritage is an impetus for mutual understanding and respect, which are the cornerstones for a united front. Awareness of the interconnectedness of social structures and norms within the Arab region also increases the potential for bonding society.

Cultural exchange projects, joint educational ventures, and common artistic undertakings are being explored as ways to celebrate individual culture while building on its sense of cultural solidarity. Furthermore, social cohesion encompasses concepts of inclusivity and civic participation that transcend historical boundaries. By fostering a spirit of society and social solidarity, Arab countries can create a common vision that demands attention for the development process. The convergence of social policies, the promotion of human rights, and the application of best practices for sustainable development are essential. The conjunction of these three aspects together weaves the social texture on which Arab society could rely for resilience and adaptability to regional challenges. A proper discourse that respects the complexities of a variety of social configurations and recognises community connectedness is crucial to creating an Arab policy that has cultural and national integrity. By embracing the complex kinesis of cultures and shared social aspirations, Arab states can mobilise the transformative potential of cultural and social cohesion to build a sustainable framework for collective action.

Addressing Security Concerns Collectively

We can develop a common Arab strategy by collectively addressing the security issue. The Arab world faces multiple security challenges. Complex and diversified security threats have characterised the geopolitical scene in the Arab world since the advent of the Arab Spring. Challenges If Arab countries develop a shared approach to security, they could de facto counter them and begin working towards long-term stability and prosperity. Security cooperation among Arab countries can vary, from intelligence exchange to training together in military exercises and building a framework for collective defence. These sorts of combined efforts help strengthen the capacity of entities across the state and serve as a deterrent against would-be aggressors. In addition, promoting a culture of trust and transparency is critical to creating security partnerships in the Arab world that will last.

This involves creating standardised mechanisms for sharing information and cooperating over emerging threat concerns. Second, maintaining peace and stability in the region, especially when addressing unconventional security threats such as cyberwar, terrorism, and cross-border crimes, requires joint vigilance and common efforts. Given the interconnected nature of these challenges, Arab states need to synchronise their efforts to checkmate these changing threats. Moreover, sharing resources for shared security infrastructure and technology can also improve overall regional resilience to newer security threats.

Strong focus on border security and cross-border enforcement is also crucial to reducing the detrimental effects of illegal activities, as well as preventing and controlling regional conflict. Moreover, a common stand against extremism and extremist ideologies also needs sustained collective action to counter terror. It also requires an end to the destruction of society in the Arab world, especially in areas where local actors collaborate with foreign powers that do not share their dependencies or vulnerabilities. Dialogue and partnerships with world powers and regional institutions create the conditions for collective response to overarching security demands. Security is a collective responsibility of the Arab world, not just a necessity; it is a chance to create lasting peace and stability. Artificial intelligence can also help the Arab world embrace and cultivate collaboration, manage competing security challenges, and become a collective force for acting together to protect the interests and welfare of all its people.

Concluding Remarks: Towards Unified Action

Finally, the need for a unified Arab approach to geopolitical changes is absolutely vital. We find that complex security, political, economic and cultural challenges and opportunities in the Arab world require a coherent response. The continuation of regional conflicts, foreign interventions and enduring internal divisions highlights the necessity of a single position. Aligning national self-interest with collective goals and setting aside old animosities and state-on-state competitions is necessary for unity of action. A common Arab approach must focus on inclusive participation and cooperation to contain destructive forces and protect the sovereignty of the region.

What it calls for is a departure from piecemeal, risky and costly reactions to shared efforts that reinforce regional stability and resistance. It also demands that leaders change their perception of security in order to pursue collective action. By focussing on cooperation in defence and intelligence sharing, joint military exercises, and shared security frameworks, it can be an effective way to deal with common threats. Through interoperability and coordination, Arab states could increase their capability to discourage aggression, the likelihood of incidents stemming from security risks, and a climate of confidence and deterrence. To reinforce the fundamental principles of unity, the Arab world must utilise its economies to establish trade partnerships, instead of squandering resources on projects that lead to mediocrity and discourage investment. These projects can serve as the foundation for a resilient economic infrastructure, enabling Arab countries to fully utilise their combined market power and resources. Fostering cultural and social cohesion, too, is essential for creating a sense of common destiny and comradery that binds the tapestry of Arab culture together in the face of modern challenges.

The importance of principled diplomacy and negotiations should be further still underscored as we traverse the road to unanimity. Crafting a common Arab position on the regional and international issues of importance requires joint diplomatic action, seeking consensus and working institutions. Diplomatic corridors ... Channels of communication have long been a vital medium for conveying common stance and mediating differences as well as for representing an Arab voice in the international forums.

In the final analysis, working for unified action calls for bold leadership, an unflinching resolution and visionary statesmanship. This is an integrated formula based on the political, economic, and security requirements of a shared vision for a prosperous and secure Arab future. In this context, the development of an Arab approach presents a positive opportunity, enabling the pursuit of a process that aims for genuine regional empowerment and invincibility.

www.ingramcontent.com/pod-product-compliance
Lightning Source LLC
Chambersburg PA
CBHW051547020426
42333CB00016B/2140